THE AUSTRALIAN Women's Weekly

People choose vegetarian food for all sorts of reasons – my interest began when I was catering to a faddish teenager, but I was soon enjoying the food for its own sake. With quick cooking methods and an almost infinite choice of fresh produce, the new vegetarian food is something the whole family will like, whether you're serving it every night or only occasionally. And because there's no time to spare when the kids say they're starving, all these dishes can be on the table in around 30 minutes.

Pamela Clark

Food Director

contents

top it off

When it comes to serving time, the difference between ho-hum and sublime vegetables can be as simple as a buttery sauce or a sprinkle of garlic breadcrumbs.

prepare-ahead flavoured butters

These prepare-ahead flavoured butters can be refrigerated up to three days, and actually improve with at least a few hours refrigeration to allow their flavours to develop. Use sparingly – 1 teaspoon per serving, melted over any combination of vegies, is sufficient.

pesto butter
Beat 125g softened butter in small bowl with electric mixer until light and creamy; stir in 1/4 cup (40g) toasted pine nuts, 1/4 cup (20g) finely grated parmesan cheese, 1/4 cup (65g) pesto and 1/2 teaspoon cracked black pepper.

tomato and olive butter
Beat 125g softened butter in small bowl with electric mixer until light and creamy; add 2 tablespoons tomato paste, 1 1/2 tablespoons chopped seeded black olives, 1 clove crushed garlic and 1/4 cup (20g) finely grated parmesan cheese.

mustard butter
Beat 125g softened butter in small bowl with electric mixer until light and creamy; stir in 2 tablespoons seeded mustard, chopped fresh chives and a little finely grated lemon rind.

curried butter
Beat 125g softened butter in small bowl with electric mixer until light and creamy; stir in 1 teaspoon mild curry powder, 1 teaspoon ground cumin, 1 clove crushed garlic and 1 tablespoon finely chopped fresh coriander.

fuss-free butter sauces

If even the simplest sauce seems like too much trouble, there are always easy melted butter sauces to give your finished dishes that special lift.

herb and lemon butter sauce
Melt about 80g butter in small saucepan; add a couple of tablespoons of freshly chopped herbs – try dill or parsley for new potatoes, for example. Stir 2 or 3 tablespoons lemon juice into the herb butter mixture and pour over hot steamed vegetables just before serving.

nut butter sauce
Melt about 80g butter in small saucepan; gently heat a couple of tablespoons of chopped nuts in the foaming butter – try hazelnuts or pine nuts on steamed green beans, or walnuts on steamed zucchini or patty-pan squash.

honeyed butter sauce
For a delicious sweet butter sauce for pumpkin, kumara or steamed carrots, melt about 80g butter in small saucepan. Add 1 tablespoon each honey and sweet chilli sauce, 1 teaspoon grated fresh ginger and 2 tablespoons water.

crispy garlic and herb breadcrumbs

Scrumptious over lightly-cooked vegetables, these crispy breadcrumbs are also a delicious addition to a risotto. Serve them sprinkled over the top, stirred through, or on the side.

Heat 1 tablespoon olive oil in large frying pan; cook 1 1/4 cups (85g) stale breadcrumbs, 1 clove crushed garlic and 1 teaspoon lemon juice over low heat, stirring, until crisp. Add 1/4 cup finely chopped fresh basil; cook, stirring, until breadcrumbs are browned lightly and very crisp.

asparagus with hollandaise sauce

ready-made toppings

Steamed green vegetables, especially broccoli, asparagus and bok choy, can be a little dull in their natural state, but they come alive when a few simple store-bought flavourings are added.

mixed seeds

These are sometimes known as "salad sprinkles". They are a mixture of sunflower and sesame seeds roasted in soy sauce with garlic. Sprinkle them over steamed vegetables (especially broccoli).

fried onion and shallot

Buy these at Asian food stores; they're chopped onions or shallots deep-fried in oil – not for kilojoule counters, but delicious sprinkled over steamed greens.

crunchy fried noodles

These are available in most supermarkets.

cashews

Or any other nuts that take your fancy, especially if roasted first then chopped.

oyster sauce

Serve over Chinese greens, broccoli or asparagus.

hollandaise sauce

Freshly steamed asparagus with hollandaise sauce is a marriage made in heaven, but not the hollandaise that takes minute after minute of whisking by hand, only to separate at the last moment into something that looks like scrambled egg. This is a no-fail, fast blender version that tastes every bit as good as the traditional one.

Combine 3 egg yolks and 2 tablespoons lemon juice in blender or food processor; pulse 5 seconds. With motor operating, pour 125g very hot melted butter into egg mixture in slow steady stream (it should take about 15 seconds). Don't use the butter's milky residue at the bottom of the saucepan. This will make about 1 cup of sauce. It can be made 1 hour ahead and kept at room temperature; reheat very gently over medium saucepan of simmering water. It's also delicious over steamed broccoli, thinly sliced steamed carrots or just-tender green beans.

lemon caper sauce

Another quick and useful sauce is lemon caper sauce. It's wonderful with baby new potatoes and adds a tasty lemony tang to mixed steamed vegies.

Heat 40g butter in small saucepan; add 1 tablespoon plain flour. Stir over heat until bubbling; remove from heat. Gradually stir in 1 cup (250ml) vegetable stock combined with 1/4 cup (60ml) lemon juice and 1/4 teaspoon sugar. Return to heat; stir until mixture boils and thickens. Stir in 1 tablespoon rinsed, drained tiny capers, 2 tablespoons finely chopped fresh flat-leaf parsley and 2 tablespoons cream.

soups

moroccan chickpea soup

PREPARATION TIME 10 MINUTES • COOKING TIME 20 MINUTES

Preserved lemons – quartered lemons preserved in salt and lemon juice – are a North African specialty. They're available from good food stores and delicatessens, but lemon juice and a little thinly sliced rind can be substituted if unavailable.

1 tablespoon olive oil
1 large brown onion (200g), chopped finely
2 cloves garlic, crushed
1 tablespoon grated fresh ginger
1¹/₂ teaspoons ground cumin
1¹/₂ teaspoons ground coriander
1 teaspoon ground turmeric
¹/₂ teaspoon sweet paprika
¹/₄ teaspoon ground cinnamon
¹/₄ cup (35g) plain flour
1 litre (4 cups) water
3 cups (750ml) vegetable stock
600g canned chickpeas, rinsed, drained
800g canned whole peeled tomatoes
1¹/₂ tablespoons finely chopped preserved lemon
1 tablespoon coarsely chopped fresh coriander

1   Heat oil in large saucepan; cook onion, garlic and ginger, stirring, until onion softens. Add spices; cook, stirring, until fragrant.

2   Add flour; cook, stirring, until mixture bubbles and thickens. Gradually stir in the water and stock; cook, stirring, until mixture boils and thickens. Reduce heat; simmer, uncovered, 5 minutes.

3   Add chickpeas and undrained crushed tomatoes; return to a boil. Reduce heat; simmer, uncovered, 10 minutes, or until soup thickens. Add lemon; stir until hot. Just before serving, stir in coriander.

SERVES 4

per serving 8.3g fat; 1044kJ

tip You could add a dash of harissa, the fiery North African condiment, to this soup if you like some extra heat.

serving suggestion Fresh or toasted pide (turkish flat bread) makes a good accompaniment for this soup.

hearty winter-vegetable soup with couscous

PREPARATION TIME 10 MINUTES • COOKING TIME 20 MINUTES

Couscous, a finely grained cereal product made from semolina, thickens this soup to a hearty consistency.

1 tablespoon olive oil
2 medium brown onions (300g),
    chopped coarsely
3 trimmed sticks celery (225g),
    chopped coarsely
1 clove garlic, crushed
1 teaspoon sweet paprika
3 medium potatoes (600g),
    chopped coarsely
2 large parsnips (360g),
    chopped coarsely
2 large carrots (360g),
    chopped coarsely
1¹/₂ cups (375ml) vegetable stock
1.25 litres (5 cups) water
¹/₂ cup (100g) couscous
2 tablespoons coarsely chopped
    fresh flat-leaf parsley

1 Heat oil in large saucepan; cook onion, celery, garlic and paprika, stirring, until onion softens.

2 Add potato, parsnip, carrot, stock and the water; bring to a boil. Reduce heat; simmer, covered, about 15 minutes or until vegetables are tender.

3 Stir in couscous and parsley; cook, uncovered, 2 minutes or until couscous is tender.

SERVES 4

per serving 5.6g fat; 1302kJ

tip Couscous should be added just before serving, as it soaks up the liquid.

serving suggestion Crusty bread and some grated or shaved parmesan are perfect accompaniments.

spinach and asparagus avgolemono

We can't vouch for its effectiveness, but there is a belief among Greek cooks that whistling when adding the egg mixture to this soup will prevent it from curdling.

1 litre (4 cups) vegetable stock
3 cups (750ml) water
1/2 cup (100g) medium-grain white rice
2 eggs, separated
1/3 cup (80ml) lemon juice
500g asparagus, chopped coarsely
1 cup (40g) loosely packed, finely shredded spinach
2 tablespoons finely chopped fresh mint

1   Bring stock and the water to a boil in large saucepan; add rice. Reduce heat; simmer, uncovered, 15 minutes, stirring occasionally.

2   Meanwhile, beat egg whites in small bowl with electric mixer until soft peaks form. Add yolks; continue beating until combined then gradually add juice.

3   Add asparagus to stock mixture; cook 1 minute or until just tender. Add spinach and mint. Remove stock mixture from heat; gradually add egg mixture, stirring constantly. Serve immediately.

SERVES 4

per serving 3.9g fat; 731kJ

tip   The stock mixture must be taken off the heat before adding egg mixture or it may curdle.

serving suggestion Serve with a Greek-style salad with fetta and olives, and warmed pitta bread for dunking.

minestrone

PREPARATION TIME 10 MINUTES • COOKING TIME 20 MINUTES

*Minestrone comes from the Italian word, minestra, which means the first course
of a meal. The name has evolved to apply to any chunky, rustic soup.*

2 teaspoons olive oil
1 small brown onion (80g), chopped coarsely
2 cloves garlic, crushed
2 trimmed sticks celery (150g), chopped coarsely
1 small carrot (70g), chopped coarsely
1 small zucchini (90g), chopped coarsely
800g canned whole peeled tomatoes
1 medium potato (200g), chopped coarsely
1¹/₂ cups (375ml) water
2¹/₂ cups (625ml) vegetable stock
1 cup (180g) macaroni
¹/₂ cup (100g) canned red kidney beans, rinsed, drained
1 cup (80g) finely shredded chinese cabbage
1 cup (40g) loosely packed, coarsely shredded spinach leaves
¹/₂ cup loosely packed, shredded fresh basil
¹/₂ cup (40g) finely grated parmesan cheese

1 Heat oil in large saucepan; cook onion and garlic, stirring occasionally,
until onion softens.

2 Add celery, carrot and zucchini; cook, stirring, 5 minutes. Stir in
undrained crushed tomatoes, potato, the water and stock; bring
to a boil. Reduce heat; simmer, uncovered, 15 minutes or until
potato is just tender.

3 Meanwhile, cook pasta in large saucepan of boiling water, uncovered,
until just tender; drain. Stir pasta and beans through soup until hot.

4 Just before serving, stir cabbage, spinach and basil into minestrone;
serve sprinkled with cheese.

SERVES 4

per serving 7.5g fat; 1456kJ

tip You can use any short pasta such as penne, small shells or elbow
macaroni in this recipe.

serving suggestion Serve this soup with warmed ciabatta, or other dense
crusty bread, and a green salad.

hot and sour soup

Straw mushrooms are a cultivated Chinese variety with an earthy flavour; they are usually sold canned in brine. Canned champignons or fresh baby button mushrooms can be substituted. A member of the ginger family, galangal has a peppery flavour.

2cm piece galangal (10g), chopped coarsely
2 tablespoons coarsely chopped lemon grass
2 green onions, chopped coarsely
3 kaffir lime leaves
1 clove garlic, quartered
2 teaspoons peanut oil
1¹/2 cups (375ml) vegetable stock
1.125 litres (4¹/2 cups) water
2cm piece fresh ginger, sliced thinly
2 red thai chillies, sliced thinly
425g canned straw mushrooms, drained, rinsed
2 teaspoons sugar
¹/3 cup (80ml) lime juice
2 teaspoons soy sauce
2 tablespoons coarsely chopped fresh coriander

1 Blend or process galangal, lemon grass, onion, lime leaves and garlic until chopped finely.

2 Heat oil in large saucepan; cook galangal mixture, stirring, until mixture is fragrant.

3 Add stock and the water; bring to a boil. Reduce heat; simmer, covered, 10 minutes. Strain stock mixture into large bowl; discard solids. Return stock mixture to same pan.

4 Return stock mixture to heat. Add ginger, chilli, mushrooms, sugar, juice and sauce; cook, uncovered, until hot. Just before serving, stir coriander through soup.

SERVES 4

per serving 3g fat; 251kJ

tips For a milder flavour, remove seeds from the chillies.
The broth can be made ahead and frozen until required.

serving suggestion Accompany soup with jasmine rice and wilted Asian greens.

pumpkin and kumara soup

PREPARATION TIME 10 MINUTES • COOKING TIME 20 MINUTES

You will need a 1.5kg piece of pumpkin for this recipe. Any type of pumpkin can be used for this soup;
we used butternut pumpkin because of its sweet flavour, sparse seed content and relatively thin skin.

40g butter
1 medium brown onion (150g),
  chopped coarsely
2 cloves garlic, crushed
2 teaspoons ground cumin
2 teaspoons ground coriander
1.1kg coarsely chopped pumpkin
1 large kumara (500g),
  chopped coarsely
1¹/₂ cups (375ml) vegetable stock
3 cups (750ml) water
¹/₄ cup (60g) sour cream
1 tablespoon finely chopped
  fresh chives

1 Melt butter in large saucepan; cook onion, garlic, cumin and coriander, stirring, until onion softens.

2 Add pumpkin, kumara, stock and the water; bring to a boil. Reduce heat; simmer, covered, about 15 minutes or until pumpkin is tender.

3 Blend or process pumpkin mixture, in batches, until smooth; return to pan.

4 Just before serving, add cream; stir over heat until mixture is hot. Serve soup topped with chives.

SERVES 4

per serving 16.1g fat; 1435kJ

tip You can buy pre-cut pumpkin to reduce preparation time.

serving suggestion This soup is great with toast or cheese muffins.

pea and potato soup

PREPARATION TIME 5 MINUTES • COOKING TIME 25 MINUTES

This is a great prepare-ahead soup which can be frozen after the processing or blending step.
Defrost in the refrigerator and, just before serving, add the cream and thyme, then reheat.

30g butter
1 small leek (200g),
  sliced thinly
2 trimmed sticks celery (150g),
  chopped coarsely
3 large potatoes (900g),
  chopped coarsely
3 cups (750ml) vegetable stock
2 cups (500ml) water
2 cups (250g) frozen peas
¹/₃ cup (80ml) cream
1 tablespoon fresh thyme

1 Melt butter in large saucepan; cook leek and celery, stirring, until vegetables soften.

2 Add potato, stock and the water. Cover; bring to a boil. Reduce heat; simmer, stirring occasionally, 15 minutes or until potato softens.

3 Add peas; cook, uncovered, about 5 minutes or until peas are tender.

4 Blend or process soup, in batches, until smooth; return to pan. Add cream and thyme; stir until hot.

SERVES 4

per serving 16.3g fat; 1476kJ

tip The smoothest consistency for this soup will be achieved by using a blender, stab mixer or mouli.

serving suggestion Serve with herb scones or crusty bread.

tortilla lime soup

PREPARATION TIME 10 MINUTES • COOKING TIME 20 MINUTES

One of the most popular soups of central Mexico, the broth and tortilla strips in this dish are fairly standard; the accompaniments, however, can vary from the onion and avocado used here to crème fraîche or sour cream, crumbled cheese – such as fetta – or crushed, fried pasilla chillies.

1 medium white onion (150g), chopped coarsely
2 cloves garlic, quartered
1 red thai chilli, chopped coarsely
4 medium tomatoes (760g), peeled, quartered
1 tablespoon peanut oil
1/4 teaspoon ground allspice
1 1/2 cups (375ml) vegetable stock
1.25 litres (5 cups) water
2 teaspoons grated lime rind
1/4 cup (60ml) lime juice
1/4 cup (70g) tomato paste
1/3 cup (80ml) peanut oil, extra
6 corn tortillas, cut into 2cm-wide strips
1 medium avocado (250g), chopped finely
2 green onions, chopped finely
1/4 cup loosely packed, coarsely chopped fresh coriander

1 Blend or process white onion, garlic, chilli and tomato until pureed.

2 Heat oil in large saucepan; cook tomato mixture and allspice, stirring, about 5 minutes or until fragrant.

3 Add stock, the water, rind, juice and paste; bring to a boil. Reduce heat; simmer, uncovered, about 15 minutes or until mixture thickens slightly.

4 Meanwhile, heat extra oil in medium frying pan; cook tortillas, in batches, until golden. Drain on absorbent paper.

5 Divide tortilla strips among bowls; ladle soup over. Top with combined avocado, green onion and coriander.

SERVES 4

per serving 26g fat; 1777kJ

serving suggestion Serve as a main dish at lunch, after a starter of guacamole and corn chips.

tips Tortilla strips can be fried a day before required and kept in an airtight container.

To reduce the fat count, crisp tortilla strips in hot oven.

lentils with caramelised onion soup

PREPARATION TIME 10 MINUTES • COOKING TIME 20 MINUTES

*Also known as bulgur wheat, burghul is hulled, steamed wheat kernels that are dried and crushed
into various sized grains to make a staple of the Middle-Eastern table.*

1¹/₂ cups (300g) red lentils
¹/₂ cup (80g) fine-grain burghul
**¹/₂ cup (100g) medium-grain
    white rice**
2 litres (8 cups) water
1 teaspoon salt
1 tablespoon ground cumin
50g butter
**3 large brown onions (600g),
    sliced thinly**
2 tablespoons sugar
3 teaspoons ground coriander
¹/₂ teaspoon cayenne pepper
**1¹/₂ cups (375ml)
    vegetable stock**

1　Rinse and drain combined lentils, burghul and rice. Bring the water to
a boil in large saucepan. Add lentils, burghul, rice, salt and cumin;
return to a boil. Reduce heat; simmer, uncovered, stirring frequently,
about 10 minutes or until lentils and grains soften.

2　Meanwhile, melt butter in large frying pan; cook onion and sugar over
medium heat, stirring, until onion begins to brown. Reduce heat; cook,
stirring, about 15 minutes or until onions are deep brown.

3　Stir coriander and cayenne into lentil mixture. Add stock; bring to a
boil. Reduce heat; simmer, uncovered, 5 minutes. Just before serving,
add caramelised onion; stir until hot.

SERVES 4

per serving 13.2g fat; 2224kJ

tips This recipe lends itself to being partially prepared in the microwave.
Combine lentils, burghul and rice in large microwave-safe bowl and cook
on HIGH (100%) for 10 minutes. Let stand 5 minutes before transferring
mixture to large saucepan and finishing the soup on the stove top.

Omit the cayenne pepper if you don't like hot foods.

serving suggestion Serve with lemon wedges.

tofu in miso broth

Wakame is a bright green lobe-leafed seaweed used in Japanese soups and salads. Miso is fermented soybean paste. White miso is a sweet variety used in salad dressings, sauces and soups. Red miso is saltier, often quite bitter in taste and popular for winter soups. Japanese pepper is also known as sansho.

1¹/2 teaspoons dashi granules
1.25 litres (5 cups) boiling water
3¹/2 tablespoons white miso
2 tablespoons red miso
1 tablespoon light soy sauce
1 tablespoon sake
150g firm tofu
30g fresh wakame
6 shiitake mushrooms,
  sliced thinly
1/2 teaspoon japanese pepper
3 green onions, sliced thinly
1 teaspoon drained pickled
  ginger, sliced thinly

1 Combine granules and the water in large heatproof bowl; stir until dissolved. Combine miso pastes and ²/3 cup (160ml) of the hot stock in small heatproof bowl; stir until blended.

2 Simmer remaining stock in medium saucepan with sauce and sake; stir in miso. Do not boil; remove from heat as soon as hot.

3 Cut tofu into 1cm cubes. Divide wakame, mushrooms, pepper and tofu evenly among serving bowls. Ladle broth into serving bowls; sprinkle with equal amounts of onion and ginger.

SERVES 4

per serving 4.7g fat; 492kJ

tip Boiling the stock after miso has been added will give this soup an unappetising, cloudy appearance.

serving suggestion Sushi would be a good appetiser to serve before this soup.

tofu noodle soup

This recipe makes enough spice paste for two soups; freeze remaining spice paste for another time.
Sambal oelek, a salty paste made from ground chillies and vinegar, is Indonesian in origin.

1 tablespoon peanut oil
1/2 cup (100g) spice paste
3 cups (750ml) water
1 litre (4 cups) vegetable stock
125g dried wheat noodles
1 cup (250ml) coconut milk
250g firm tofu, cut into 1cm cubes
1 cup (80g) bean sprouts
4 green onions, chopped finely
2 tablespoons coarsely chopped fresh mint

SPICE PASTE
1 cup loosely packed, coarsely chopped fresh coriander
2 green onions, chopped coarsely
1 tablespoon ground coriander
1 tablespoon ground cumin
2 teaspoons ground turmeric
2 cloves garlic, quartered
2 tablespoons sambal oelek
2 teaspoons grated fresh ginger
1 stalk lemon grass, chopped coarsely

1   Heat oil in large saucepan; cook spice paste, stirring, 1 minute or until fragrant.

2   Add the water and stock. Bring to a boil; add noodles. Reduce heat; simmer, uncovered, 5 minutes or until noodles are just tender.

3   Add coconut milk and tofu to soup; stir until hot. Add bean sprouts, onion and mint.

spice paste Blend or process ingredients until smooth.

SERVES 4

per serving 23.7g fat; 1644kJ

tip This soup is best made just before serving.

serving suggestion Add other Asian green vegetables, such as coarsely chopped baby bok choy, when adding sprouts.

asian mushroom broth

Other varieties of mushrooms, such as button or shimeji, can also be used in this recipe.

cooking-oil spray
4 green onions, chopped finely
1 trimmed stick celery (75g), chopped finely
1.5 litres (6 cups) vegetable stock
1¹/₂ cups (375ml) water
¹/₄ cup (60ml) light soy sauce
100g shiitake mushrooms, sliced thinly
100g enoki mushrooms, trimmed
150g oyster mushrooms, sliced thinly
150g swiss brown mushrooms, sliced thinly
¹/₂ teaspoon five-spice powder
2 tablespoons finely chopped fresh garlic chives

1 Spray heated large saucepan with cooking-oil spray; cook onion and celery, stirring, until vegetables soften.

2 Add stock, the water and sauce; bring to a boil. Add mushrooms and five-spice; return to a boil. Reduce heat; simmer 2 minutes or until mushrooms soften. Just before serving, sprinkle with chives.

SERVES 4

per serving 2.7g fat; 374kJ

tip Dried shiitake mushrooms can be used instead of fresh.
Place mushrooms in small heatproof bowl; cover with boiling water.
Stand 20 minutes; drain. Discard stems; slice caps thinly.

serving suggestion Serve with a starter of stuffed tofu pouches to make a more substantial meal.

dips

Whether served with drinks as an informal first course, or as an anytime snack, dips are a delicious way to add extra nutrition and variety to a vegetarian diet.

chile con queso

PREPARATION TIME 10 MINUTES
COOKING TIME 5 MINUTES

We used fontina but any good melting cheese can be used. Make just before serving as it will set as it cools.

- **1 cup (125g) grated fontina cheese**
- **1 tablespoon finely chopped bottled jalapeño peppers**
- **1/2 small white onion (40g), chopped finely**
- **1 teaspoon ground cumin**

1 Combine ingredients in small saucepan; cook, stirring, over medium heat until cheese melts. Serve immediately.

MAKES 1/2 CUP

per tablespoon 7.1g fat; 370kJ

tip Serve dip in fondue pot over a burner to stop it from setting as it cools.

serving suggestion Serve with corn chips or shards of oven-baked flour tortillas.

spinach, cheese and onion dip

PREPARATION TIME 10 MINUTES
COOKING TIME 5 MINUTES

This flavour-packed dip is inspired by the Greek mezethes platter.

- **70g baby spinach leaves**
- **2 teaspoons olive oil**
- **6 green onions, chopped coarsely**
- **1 clove garlic, quartered**
- **250g ricotta cheese**
- **250g fetta cheese**
- **2 tablespoons lemon juice**

1 Boil, steam or microwave spinach until just wilted; drain. Cool; chop finely.

2 Blend or process spinach with remaining ingredients until almost smooth.

MAKES 2 CUPS

per tablespoon 4g fat; 207kJ

tip Frozen spinach can be substituted for fresh leaves, if preferred.

serving suggestion Serve with rice crackers, dolmades (stuffed vine leaves), olives and raw vegetable sticks for dipping.

caraway and caper dip

PREPARATION TIME 5 MINUTES

The combination of cream cheese, caraway and capers owes its origin to the Hungarian dip, liptauer.

- **250g cream cheese**
- **1 tablespoon drained baby capers**
- **1 teaspoon caraway seeds**
- **1 teaspoon sweet paprika**
- **1/4 cup (60g) sour cream**

1 Combine ingredients in small bowl; mix well.

MAKES 1 1/2 CUPS

per tablespoon 6g fat; 255kJ

tip Dip can be made several days ahead and refrigerated, covered.

serving suggestion Serve with crackers or carrot and celery sticks.

watercress and yogurt dip

PREPARATION TIME 5 MINUTES

This dip also makes a great topping for steamed vegetables or soups.

400g watercress, trimmed
200g yogurt
2 cloves garlic, quartered

1 Blend or process ingredients until smooth.

MAKES 1¼ CUPS

per tablespoon 0.6g fat; 63kJ
tip Dip should be made just before serving as the watercress can discolour.
serving suggestion Serve with pide (turkish bread) or rice crackers.

sesame and butter bean dip

PREPARATION TIME 8 MINUTES

This dip is typical of the offerings which make up the array of appetisers served at eastern Mediterranean tables.

600g canned butter beans, rinsed, drained
2 teaspoons ground cumin
2 tablespoons lemon juice
1 tablespoon sesame seeds, toasted
2 tablespoons olive oil

1 Blend or process ingredients until smooth.

MAKES 2 CUPS

per tablespoon 1.8g fat; 85kJ
tip Dip can be made a day ahead and refrigerated, covered.
serving suggestion Serve with crackers, bagel chips or crisped pitta bread.

mexican bean layer dip

PREPARATION TIME 20 MINUTES

This makes a good prepare-ahead dish for a picnic, party or barbecue.

450g canned refried beans
½ cup (160g) mild tomato salsa
1 cup (125g) coarsely grated cheddar cheese
2 medium avocados (500g)
1 tablespoon lemon juice
1 small tomato (130g), chopped finely
½ small red onion (50g), chopped finely
2 tablespoons finely chopped fresh coriander
½ cup (120g) sour cream
pinch cayenne pepper

1 Combine beans and salsa in small bowl. Spread over base of 1.5-litre (6 cup) serving dish.

2 Sprinkle bean mixture with cheese.

3 Mash avocado in medium bowl until almost smooth. Stir in juice, tomato, onion and coriander. Spread avocado mixture over cheese. Top with sour cream; sprinkle with cayenne pepper.

MAKES 6 CUPS

per tablespoon 2.4g fat; 125kJ
tip Dip can be made a day ahead and refrigerated, covered.
serving suggestion Serve with corn chips or cracker biscuits.

spinach, cheese and onion dip

snacks

carrot and zucchini noodle rolls

PREPARATION TIME 20 MINUTES

You will need about two medium carrots (240g) and three small zucchini (270g) for this recipe.

1 cup loosely packed, coarsely grated carrot
1^1/$_3$ cups loosely packed, coarsely grated zucchini
2 green onions, chopped finely
1 tablespoon light soy sauce
1 tablespoon sweet chilli sauce
^{1}/$_2$ teaspoon sesame oil
^{1}/$_2$ teaspoon grated fresh ginger
8 x 22cm rice paper sheets

1 Combine carrot, zucchini, onion, sauces, oil and ginger in medium bowl.

2 Place one sheet of rice paper in medium bowl of warm water until softened slightly; lift sheet carefully from water. Place on board; pat dry with absorbent paper.

3 Divide carrot mixture into eight portions; place one portion in centre of rice paper sheet. Roll to enclose filling, folding in sides after first complete turn of the roll. Repeat with remaining rice sheets and filling.

SERVES 4

per serving 1.2g fat; 398kJ

tip You can also use fresh rice noodle sheets, cut into 14cm x 16cm rectangles, to enclose the filling.

serving suggestion Serve with a snow pea sprout salad.

italian-style sandwich

PREPARATION TIME 10 MINUTES • COOKING TIME 5 MINUTES

*Pide, also known as Turkish bread, comes in long (about 45cm) flat loaves as well as individual rounds.
It is made from wheat flour and sprinkled with sesame or black onion seeds.*

1 long loaf pide
1/4 cup (65g) basil pesto
2 x 280g jars char-grilled
vegetables in oil, drained
1/3 cup loosely packed fresh basil

1 Quarter bread; split pieces horizontally. Grill or toast on both sides until browned lightly.

2 Spread four bread halves with equal amounts of pesto; top each slice with equal amounts of vegetables and basil. Cover each sandwich with remaining toast halves.

SERVES 4

per serving 21.4g fat; 1790kJ

tips You can make your own pesto for this recipe.

Char-grilled vegetables can be purchased in supermarkets or delicatessens.

serving suggestion You could add sun-dried tomatoes and shaved parmesan to the filling, if desired.

ratatouille-stuffed potatoes

PREPARATION TIME 15 MINUTES • COOKING TIME 20 MINUTES

Pontiac, desiree or spunta potatoes are great for cooking in their jackets.

8 large potatoes (2.4kg)
1 tablespoon olive oil
1 small brown onion (80g),
　　chopped coarsely
1 clove garlic, crushed
1/2 small red capsicum (75g),
　　chopped coarsely
1 small zucchini (90g),
　　chopped coarsely
1 baby eggplant (60g),
　　chopped coarsely
100g button mushrooms,
　　quartered
400g canned whole
　　peeled tomatoes
1/4 cup (70g) tomato paste
1/2 cup (60g) coarsely grated
　　cheddar cheese

1　Prick skin of potatoes in several places; place on absorbent paper around edge of microwave oven turntable. Cook potatoes, uncovered, on HIGH (100%) about 12 minutes or until potatoes are tender.

2　Meanwhile, heat oil in medium frying pan; cook onion and garlic until onion softens. Add capsicum, zucchini, eggplant and mushrooms; cook, stirring, until just tender.

3　Stir in undrained crushed tomatoes and paste; bring to a boil. Reduce heat; simmer, uncovered, until ratatouille mixture thickens slightly.

4　Cut off a third from the top of each potato. Scoop out flesh from potatoes, leaving 1cm-thick shell; discard tops and flesh, or use in another recipe.

5　Spoon ratatouille into shells; top with cheese. Place on absorbent paper around edge of microwave turntable; cook, uncovered, on MEDIUM (55%) about 3 minutes or until cheese melts.

SERVES 4

per serving　10.7g fat; 2273kJ

tip　You could oven-bake your potatoes but it will take about 1 1/2 hours.

serving suggestion　Serve with a green leaf salad and dressing made with balsamic vinegar.

tempeh sang choy bow

Tempeh is a meat alternative made from fermented soy beans.

1 tablespoon vegetable oil
2 cloves garlic, crushed
1 medium carrot (120g), grated coarsely
100g mushrooms, chopped coarsely
227g canned bamboo shoots, drained, sliced thinly
4 green onions, chopped finely
300g tempeh, chopped finely
2 tablespoons hoisin sauce
2 tablespoons light soy sauce
8 iceberg lettuce leaves

1 Heat oil in large wok or heavy-based frying pan; stir-fry garlic, carrot, mushrooms and bamboo shoots about 2 minutes or until vegetables just soften.

2 Add onion and tempeh; stir-fry until tempeh is hot.

3 Add sauces to wok; stir to combine. To serve, divide tempeh mixture among lettuce leaves.

SERVES 4

per serving 9.1g fat; 803kJ

tip Add some crispy fried noodles to tempeh mixture.

serving suggestion Serve with bowls of chilli and soy sauce, to be added to taste.

rocket and butter bean bruschetta

PREPARATION TIME 10 MINUTES • COOKING TIME 5 MINUTES

You can use any densely textured, crusty Italian-style bread rolls in this recipe.

2 bread rolls
2 tablespoons olive oil
1/3 cup (90g) olive paste
60g rocket, shredded coarsely
2 medium egg tomatoes (150g),
   chopped finely
300g canned butter beans,
   rinsed, drained
1/4 cup loosely packed, coarsely
   chopped fresh coriander
1 small red onion (100g),
   chopped finely

1 Cut rolls in half horizontally. Brush cut sides with oil; toast on both sides.

2 Spread the cut side of each half with equal amounts of paste; top with equal amounts of combined rocket, tomato, beans, coriander and onion.

SERVES 4

per serving 10.3g fat; 796kJ

tip This topping also makes a good focaccia filling.

serving suggestion You could add some chopped seeded olives to the bruschetta topping mixture.

lentil burger with tahini dressing

PREPARATION TIME 20 MINUTES (plus refrigeration time) • COOKING TIME 10 MINUTES

Tahini, a rich, buttery paste made from crushed sesame seeds, lends its distinctive tang to the dressing on these burgers.

400g canned brown lentils,
   rinsed, drained
1 tablespoon vegetable oil
1 medium brown onion (150g),
   chopped finely
1 tablespoon grated fresh ginger
2 cloves garlic, crushed
2 teaspoons ground coriander
2 teaspoons ground cumin
1/4 cup loosely packed, coarsely
   chopped fresh coriander
2 eggs, beaten lightly
2 cups (140g) stale breadcrumbs
4 bread rolls
1 large carrot (180g)
vegetable oil, for shallow-frying
1 cup (40g) alfalfa sprouts
1 small red onion (100g),
   sliced thinly

TAHINI DRESSING
1/4 cup (70g) tahini
1/4 cup (60ml) lemon juice
2 tablespoons water

1 Blend or process lentils until smooth.

2 Heat oil in medium frying pan; cook onion, ginger and garlic, stirring, until onion softens. Add ground coriander and cumin; cook, stirring, until fragrant.

3 Combine lentil puree, onion mixture, fresh coriander, eggs and half of the breadcrumbs in medium bowl; mix well. Using hands, shape mixture into four patties. Dip patties in remaining breadcrumbs; turn to coat all sides. Shake off excess; refrigerate at least 10 minutes.

4 Meanwhile, split each bread roll horizontally; toast both sides. Using vegetable peeler, slice carrot into ribbons.

5 Heat oil in large frying pan; cook patties about 5 minutes or until browned on both sides. Drain on absorbent paper.

6 Place patties on bottom half of rolls; divide carrot, sprouts, onion and tahini dressing among lentil burgers. Top with remaining halves.

tahini dressing Combine ingredients in small bowl; mix well.

SERVES 4

per serving 38.6g fat; 2655kJ

tip Uncooked patties and tahini dressing can be prepared in advance and refrigerated, covered, until just before serving.

serving suggestion Some char-grilled eggplant or zucchini can be added to the burger fillings.

mushroom pizza

PREPARATION TIME 10 MINUTES • COOKING TIME 15 MINUTES

We used packaged pizza bases measuring 15cm across for this recipe, but any fresh or frozen variety would also be suitable. Pizza cheese is a commercial blend of mozzarella, parmesan and cheddar. You might prefer to substitute your own blend of cheeses.

4 x 112g pizza bases
1¹/₂ cups (185g) grated pizza cheese
150g flat mushrooms, sliced thinly
100g fetta cheese, crumbled
2 tablespoons finely chopped fresh chives

1 Preheat oven to hot. Place pizza bases on oven tray. Divide pizza cheese into four portions; sprinkle half of each portion over each base. Divide mushrooms, fetta cheese, chives and remaining pizza cheese among bases.

2 Bake, uncovered, in hot oven 15 minutes or until pizza tops are browned lightly and bases are crisp.

SERVES 4

per serving 22.1g fat; 2325kJ

tip We used a Greek fetta which crumbles well and has a sharp taste.

serving suggestion Serve with a salad of rocket, olives and fresh or slow-roasted tomatoes.

rolled omelette with fresh tomato salsa

PREPARATION TIME 15 MINUTES • COOKING TIME 10 MINUTES

Eggs are the short-order cook's greatest ally – here, they come to the rescue in a savoury-filled omelette.

8 eggs
²/₃ cup (160ml) milk
**1 small red onion (100g),
    chopped coarsely**
**4 small tomatoes (520g),
    chopped coarsely**
**1 medium avocado (250g),
    chopped coarsely**
**¹/₄ cup loosely packed, coarsely
    chopped fresh coriander**
1 clove garlic, crushed
2 tablespoons lime juice

1 Combine eggs and milk in medium bowl; whisk until smooth.

2 Heat oiled small frying pan; pour in a quarter of the egg mixture. Cover; cook over medium heat until omelette sets. Remove from pan; keep warm. Repeat with remaining egg mixture.

3 Combine remaining ingredients in medium bowl; mix well.

4 Place a quarter of the tomato salsa mixture on edge of one omelette; roll up carefully. Repeat with remaining omelettes and salsa.

SERVES 4

per serving 22.2g fat; 1235kJ

tip Salsa can be made several hours in advance if avocado is omitted until just before serving time.

serving suggestion This makes a great brunch dish, or add a green salad on the side for a flavour-packed light lunch.

felafel and salad roll

Felafel mix is a packaged combination of ground chickpeas, herbs and spices which, when combined with water, makes a full-flavoured patty for rolls and burgers.

400g packet felafel mix
vegetable oil, for shallow-frying
1 medium avocado (250g)
1 teaspoon lemon juice
1/2 cup (150g) mayonnaise
1/2 small red onion (50g),
   chopped coarsely
1 medium tomato (190g),
   chopped coarsely
8 lettuce leaves, torn
4 large pitta

1 Make felafel according to instructions on packet. Shape level tablespoons of mixture into patties.

2 Heat oil in medium frying pan; cook felafel, in batches, until browned on both sides. Drain on absorbent paper.

3 Mash avocado, juice and mayonnaise in small bowl. Add onion and tomato; mix well.

4 Divide lettuce and avocado mixture among pittas; top with felafel. Roll pittas to enclose filling.

SERVES 4

per serving 66.1g fat; 5794kJ

tip Nugget mix can be substituted for felafel mix, if preferred.

serving suggestion Add other salad ingredients, such as carrot or bean sprouts, and some smoky barbecue sauce to these rolls.

empanadas

Empanadas are sweet or savoury turnovers made from flaky pastry. Our quick savoury version uses ready-rolled puff pastry sheets.

1 tablespoon vegetable oil

1 small brown onion (80g), chopped coarsely

2 small tomatoes (260g), seeded, chopped coarsely

1 small green capsicum (150g), chopped coarsely

2 tablespoons drained, thinly sliced, seeded black olives

2 tablespoons coarsely chopped fresh flat-leaf parsley

3 sheets ready-rolled puff pastry, thawed

1¹/₂ cups (185g) coarsely grated cheddar cheese

1 Heat oil in medium frying pan; cook onion, tomato, capsicum and olives, stirring, until tomato just begins to soften. Remove from heat; stir through parsley. Allow filling to cool.

2 Preheat oven to moderately hot. Using 11cm-round cutter, cut four rounds from each pastry sheet.

3 Divide tomato filling among pastry rounds; top with equal amounts of cheese. Fold over pastry to enclose filling; pinch edges together to seal. Using knife, make two 1cm cuts in each pastry top.

4 Place empanadas on greased oven tray; bake in moderately hot oven 15 minutes or until golden.

MAKES 12

per empanada 16.3g fat; 934kJ

tip Filling can be prepared in advance and refrigerated, covered, until just before baking.

serving suggestion Serve with an avocado salad, or guacamole and sweet chilli sauce.

bean nachos

Mexican-style beans are a mildly spiced, canned combination of red kidney or pinto beans, capsicum and tomato.

420g canned Mexican-style beans, drained

290g canned red kidney beans, rinsed, drained, mashed

2 tablespoons tomato paste

1 tablespoon water

230g packet plain corn chips

1¹/₂ cups (185g) coarsely grated cheddar cheese

1 large avocado (320g)

1 small red onion (100g), chopped finely

1 large tomato (250g), chopped finely

1 teaspoon lemon juice

¹/₂ cup (120g) sour cream

1 tablespoon coarsely chopped fresh coriander

1 Preheat oven to moderately hot. Heat combined beans, paste and the water, stirring, in large non-stick frying pan. Cover; keep warm.

2 Place corn chips in large ovenproof dish; sprinkle with cheese. Bake in moderately hot oven 5 minutes or until cheese melts.

3 Meanwhile, mash avocado in small bowl; stir in half of the combined onion and tomato, and juice.

4 Top heated corn chips with bean mixture, avocado mixture and sour cream; sprinkle nachos with remaining onion and tomato, and coriander.

SERVES 4

per serving 60g fat; 3840kJ

tips Drizzle sweet chilli sauce over sour cream for a spicy alternative.

Corn chips are available in a variety of flavours, any of which can be substituted for the plain variety.

serving suggestion Serve as an appetiser to chickpea corn enchiladas (page 52).

mini muffin dampers

These little dampers would make a good accompaniment for soups or savoury dishes with lots of sauce to be mopped up.

3 cups (450g) self-raising flour
40g butter, chopped coarsely
1³/₄ cups (430ml) buttermilk
2 tablespoons basil pesto
³/₄ cup (90g) coarsely grated cheddar cheese
¹/₄ teaspoon sweet paprika
1 tablespoon plain flour

1   Preheat oven to moderately hot. Grease 12-hole (¹/₃ cup/80ml) muffin pan.

2   Place self-raising flour in large bowl; rub in butter with fingertips. Using fork, stir in buttermilk to form a soft but sticky dough. Swirl pesto and cheese through; do not overmix.

3   Divide mixture among holes of prepared pan. Sprinkle with combined paprika and flour.

4   Bake in moderately hot oven about 25 minutes.

5   Stand dampers in pan 5 minutes before turning out onto wire rack.

MAKES 12

per damper 7.8g fat; 929kJ

tip Use bottled pesto to save time. A sun-dried tomato pesto can also be used.

serving suggestion Dampers are great served warm with tomato relish.

eggs poached in pungent sauce

PREPARATION TIME 10 MINUTES • COOKING TIME 10 MINUTES

*Most Mediterranean cuisines have a version of this dish, although this recipe
owes its inspiration to the kitchens of Morocco.*

2 tablespoons olive oil

6 cloves garlic, crushed

1 tablespoon sweet paprika

1¹/₂ teaspoons ground cumin

1 teaspoon caraway seeds

¹/₂ teaspoon cayenne pepper

800g canned whole
peeled tomatoes

1 cup (250ml) water

1 long loaf pide

8 eggs

1 tablespoon coarsely chopped
fresh coriander

1 tablespoon coarsely chopped
fresh parsley

1 Heat oil in large frying pan; cook garlic, stirring, 1 minute. Add paprika, cumin, seeds and cayenne; cook, stirring, until fragrant. Blend or process undrained tomatoes until smooth. Add tomato and the water to pan; bring to a boil. Reduce heat; simmer, stirring occasionally, 10 minutes.

2 Meanwhile, cut pide into four even pieces. Split each piece horizontally; toast on both sides.

3 Just before serving, break eggs into simmering sauce; cover pan. Turn off heat; stand about 3 minutes, or until a light film of egg white has set over yolks.

4 Divide pungent sauce among toasted pide. Top each slice with an egg; sprinkle with coriander and parsley.

SERVES 4

per serving 22.7g fat; 2018kJ

tip Sauce can be made in advance and refrigerated, covered, until just before serving.

serving suggestion This also makes an unusual breakfast dish. Reduce the quantity of cayenne if you prefer milder flavours at this time of day.

spanish tortilla

Canned tiny new potatoes are a nifty shortcut in this recipe.

1 tablespoon olive oil

1 large brown onion (200g), sliced thinly

750g canned tiny new potatoes, drained, sliced thickly

6 eggs, beaten lightly

100g fetta cheese, chopped coarsely

1/3 cup (25g) finely grated parmesan cheese

1/3 cup (40g) coarsely grated cheddar cheese

1 Heat oil in medium frying pan; cook onion, stirring, until onion softens.

2 Combine onion, potato, eggs and cheeses in large bowl.

3 Pour potato mixture into heated oiled medium non-stick frying pan. Cover; cook over low heat 10 minutes or until egg sets.

4 Carefully invert tortilla onto plate and slide back into frying pan. Cook further 5 minutes or until cooked through.

5 Remove from heat; allow to cool in pan.

SERVES 4

per serving 23.8g fat; 1560kJ

tip Tortilla can be eaten hot or cold and makes great picnic fare.

serving suggestion Serve with a salad of orange, red onion, olives and tomatoes, or a plain rocket salad.

tofu burger

PREPARATION TIME 10 MINUTES • COOKING TIME 5 MINUTES

Kecap manis is an Indonesian thick soy sauce which has sugar and spices added.

375g firm tofu
1/4 cup (60ml) kecap manis
1 tablespoon peanut oil
2 medium brown onions
   (300g), sliced thinly
4 wholegrain bread rolls, halved
4 iceberg lettuce leaves
2 medium tomatoes (380g),
   sliced thickly
1 medium avocado (250g),
   sliced thickly
1 tablespoon barbecue sauce

1 Slice tofu horizontally into four pieces; cut each piece in half lengthways. Place tofu in large bowl; coat with kecap manis.

2 Heat oil in medium frying pan; cook tofu, in batches, until browned on both sides and heated through.

3 Add onion to pan; cook, stirring, until onion browns.

4 Meanwhile, grill cut sides of bread until browned lightly.

5 Place lettuce on bottom half of rolls. Top with tomato, tofu, onion, avocado and sauce; top with remaining halves.

SERVES 4

per serving 22.2g fat; 1555kJ

tips You can use your favourite bread instead of the wholegrain rolls. Tofu can be marinated overnight, if desired.

serving suggestion Serve with potato wedges and sweet chilli sauce.

potato and rosemary pizza

PREPARATION TIME 8 MINUTES • COOKING TIME 15 MINUTES

For this recipe we used packaged pizza bases, which measure 15cm across and come in packs of two, but any fresh or frozen variety would also be suitable.

4 x 112g pizza bases
1 1/2 cups (120g) finely grated
   parmesan cheese
3 tiny new potatoes (120g)
1 tablespoon coarsely chopped
   fresh rosemary
3 cloves garlic, sliced thinly

1 Preheat oven to hot. Place pizza bases on oven tray. Divide half of the cheese into four portions; sprinkle a portion over each pizza base.

2 Slice potatoes thinly using vegetable peeler; divide into four portions. Layer a portion of potato over cheese-topped base in circular pattern until covered; repeat with remaining potato and bases. Divide rosemary and garlic among bases. Sprinkle remaining cheese evenly over pizzas.

3 Bake, uncovered, in hot oven 15 minutes or until pizza tops are browned lightly and bases are crisp.

SERVES 4

per serving 9.8g fat; 647kJ

tip You could use one large packaged pizza base instead of making individual servings.

serving suggestion Serve with a tossed green salad.

nibbles

Why snack on junk food when healthier alternatives can be so delicious? When the munchies strike, be ready with a selection of these quick and easy nibbles.

apricot chews

PREPARATION TIME 10 MINUTES
COOKING TIME 10 MINUTES

To toast sesame seeds, place in small frying pan over medium heat and cook, stirring, until seeds brown lightly.

- **1/2 cup (75g) coarsely chopped dried apricots**
- **1/4 cup (60ml) orange juice**
- **2 tablespoons honey**
- **1/2 cup (50g) skim milk powder**
- **1/2 cup (80g) almond kernels, chopped coarsely**
- **1 tablespoon sesame seeds, toasted**
- **1 teaspoon finely grated orange rind**
- **1/2 cup (75g) currants**
- **1/4 cup (20g) desiccated coconut**
- **1/2 cup (55g) natural muesli**
- **1/2 cup (45g) desiccated coconut, toasted, extra**

1 Combine apricots, juice and honey in small saucepan; bring to a boil. Reduce heat; simmer, uncovered, 10 minutes or until apricots are tender, cool.

2 Stir in remaining ingredients, except extra coconut. Roll rounded tablespoons of mixture into balls; roll in extra coconut. Place apricot chews on baking-paper-lined tray; refrigerate about 30 minutes or until set.

MAKES 18

per chew 5.4g fat; 429kJ
tip Dried peaches or pears can be substituted for apricots, if preferred.

parmesan crisps

PREPARATION TIME 10 MINUTES
COOKING TIME 5 MINUTES
(plus standing time)

- **2 cups (160g) finely grated parmesan cheese**
- **1/2 teaspoon chilli powder**
- **2 teaspoons finely grated lemon rind**
- **1 tablespoon finely chopped fresh coriander**

1 Preheat oven to moderately hot.

2 Combine half of the cheese with chilli powder in small bowl.

3 Combine remaining cheese with rind and coriander in another small bowl.

4 Place tablespoons of chilli mixture onto oiled oven trays. Bake in moderately hot oven about 5 minutes or until browned lightly. Stand 2 minutes; cool crisps on wire rack. Repeat with lemon cheese mixture.

MAKES 24

per crisp 2.2g fat; 124kJ
tip Crisps can be made a day ahead and stored in an airtight container.

peanut butter twists

chilli popcorn

PREPARATION TIME 5 MINUTES
COOKING TIME 5 MINUTES

Here, we give the perennially popular cinema snack an injection of spice.

- **2 tablespoons vegetable oil**
- **1 cup (230g) popping corn**
- **60g butter**
- **1/2 teaspoon cayenne pepper**
- **1/2 teaspoon hot paprika**
- **1 teaspoon salt**

1 Heat oil in large heavy-based saucepan; cook popcorn, covered, until corn stops popping. Place popcorn in large serving bowl.

2 Melt butter in small saucepan. Add cayenne pepper, paprika and salt; stir to combine.

3 Pour butter mixture over popcorn and toss well to coat.

MAKES 13 CUPS

per 1/2-cup serving 3.7g fat; 239kJ
tip Reduce or eliminate the butter for a lower-fat alternative.

tapenade pinwheels

PREPARATION TIME 10 MINUTES
COOKING TIME 20 MINUTES

- **1/2 cup (60g) seeded black olives**
- **1 tablespoon drained capers**
- **1/4 cup (50g) drained, coarsely chopped, sun-dried capsicums in oil**
- **2 tablespoons olive oil**
- **2 sheets ready-rolled puff pastry**

1 Preheat oven to moderately hot.

2 Blend or process olives, capers, capsicum and oil until mixture is almost smooth.

3 Spread each sheet of pastry with olive mixture; roll pastry up, enclosing filling. Cut roll into 2cm slices.

4 Place slices on oiled oven trays; bake pinwheels in moderately hot oven about 20 minutes or until browned and crisp.

MAKES 24

per pinwheel 4.9g fat; 305kJ

tips Pinwheels can be made a day ahead and stored in an airtight container.

Sun-dried tomatoes can be substituted for capsicum, if preferred.

peanut butter twists

PREPARATION TIME 10 MINUTES
COOKING TIME 15 MINUTES

You will need to thaw the pastry sheets on a wire rack for about 10 minutes.

- **1/3 cup (95g) crunchy peanut butter**
- **2 sheets ready-rolled puff pastry**
- **1/3 cup (25g) finely grated parmesan cheese**
- **1 tablespoon sesame seeds**

1 Preheat oven to moderate.

2 Spread peanut butter evenly over both sheets of pastry; sprinkle with cheese and seeds.

3 Cut pastry into 1cm strips; fold each strip in half with filling on the inside. Holding both ends, twist pastry gently.

4 Place twists on lightly oiled oven tray. Bake in moderate oven about 15 minutes or until twists are golden and crisp; cool on tray.

MAKES 48

per twist 2.9g fat; 172kJ

tip Store crisps in an airtight container in the fridge; reheat in a moderate oven for 5 minutes.

serving suggestion These are great for lunch boxes or snacks after school.

fruit and nut mix

PREPARATION TIME 10 MINUTES

You can vary the types and proportions of dried fruits to suit your personal preference, or add some coarsely chopped dark chocolate to make a version of the high-energy bushwalker's treat known as scroggin.

- **1/4 cup (35g) dried apricots, chopped coarsely**
- **1/4 cup (35g) dried peaches, chopped coarsely**
- **1/4 cup (35g) dried pears, chopped coarsely**
- **1/4 cup (55g) dried pineapple, chopped coarsely**
- **1/4 cup (35g) dried mango, chopped coarsely**
- **1/4 cup (40g) pitted dates, chopped coarsely**
- **1/4 cup (40g) blanched whole almonds**
- **1/4 cup (25g) walnut halves**
- **1/4 cup (40g) sultanas**

1 Combine ingredients in medium bowl; mix well.

SERVES 4

per serving 11g fat; 1144kJ

tip Add jelly beans to the mix for a colourful variation.

serving suggestion This mix makes a welcome addition to the school or work lunch box.

mains

fettuccine with rocket pesto and fresh tomato salsa

PREPARATION TIME 10 MINUTES • COOKING TIME 15 MINUTES

500g fettuccine
8 cloves garlic, quartered
1/2 cup loosely packed, coarsely chopped fresh basil
120g rocket, chopped coarsely
2/3 cup (160ml) olive oil
1/2 cup (40g) finely grated parmesan cheese
3 medium tomatoes (570g), chopped coarsely
2 tablespoons lemon juice
2 red thai chillies, sliced thinly
1/3 cup (50g) pine nuts, toasted

1 Cook pasta in a large saucepan of boiling water, uncovered, until just tender; drain.

2 Meanwhile, blend or process garlic, basil, rocket and oil until smooth.

3 Combine pasta, rocket pesto, cheese, tomato, juice and chilli in large saucepan; cook, stirring, until hot. Add nuts, toss gently to combine.

SERVES 4

per serving 50.3g fat; 3780kJ

tip You could substitute baby spinach leaves for the rocket for a milder-flavoured pesto.

serving suggestion Serve an appetiser of olive and tomato bruschetta before the pasta.

stir-fried vegetables with rice noodles

PREPARATION TIME 15 MINUTES • COOKING TIME 10 MINUTES

You will need about 300g broccoli to make the florets for this recipe.

250g dried rice noodles
1 tablespoon peanut oil
1 teaspoon sesame oil
1 large brown onion (200g),
  sliced thickly
1 clove garlic, crushed
1/4 cup (60ml) light soy sauce
1/3 cup (80ml) sweet chilli sauce
1/2 cup (125ml) water
2 teaspoons grated fresh ginger
1 tablespoon sweet sherry
2 teaspoons cornflour
2 tablespoons water, extra
1 medium red capsicum (200g),
  chopped coarsely
180g broccoli florets
150g snow peas, halved lengthways
425g can baby corn cuts, drained,
  halved lengthways

1 Place noodles in medium heatproof bowl, cover with boiling water, stand until tender; drain.

2 Meanwhile, heat oils in wok or large frying pan; stir-fry onion and garlic until onion softens. Add sauces, the water, ginger and sherry; bring to a boil. Blend cornflour and the extra water, add to wok; stir until sauce boils and thickens.

3 Add capsicum, broccoli, snow peas and corn; stir-fry until vegetables are just tender.

4 Serve noodles with stir-fried vegetables.

SERVES 4

per serving 8g fat; 1609kJ

tip This dish is best made just before serving. You can vary the vegetables according to your taste and what's in season.

serving suggestion Serve tempeh sang choy bow (page 30) as a starter before this dish.

mushroom stroganoff

PREPARATION TIME 10 MINUTES • COOKING TIME 15 MINUTES

The meat-eaters' version of this dish includes beef or veal and is said to have been prepared as an after-theatre supper for a member of the Russian nobility; in fact, variants of it exist in most Baltic countries.

250g fettuccine
30g butter
1 large brown onion (200g),
   chopped coarsely
1 clove garlic, crushed
400g flat mushrooms,
   chopped coarsely
200g swiss brown
   mushrooms, quartered
150g shiitake mushrooms,
   quartered
150g oyster mushrooms, halved
1/4 cup (60ml) red wine
1 cup (250ml) bottled tomato
   pasta sauce
1 cup (250ml) vegetable stock
1/2 cup (125ml) water
1 tablespoon cornflour
1/4 cup (60ml) water, extra
1/2 cup (120g) sour cream
1/4 cup loosely packed, coarsely
   chopped fresh flat-leaf parsley

1 Cook pasta in large saucepan of boiling water, uncovered, until just tender; drain.

2 Meanwhile, melt butter in large saucepan, add onion and garlic; cook, stirring, until onion softens. Add mushrooms; cook, stirring, until mushrooms are browned and just tender. Add wine, sauce, stock and the water, bring to a boil; reduce heat, simmer 5 minutes.

3 Blend cornflour and the extra water in a small jug, add to mushroom mixture; cook, stirring, until sauce boils and thickens. Add sour cream and parsley; stir until hot. Serve mushroom stroganoff with pasta.

SERVES 4

per serving 20.3g fat; 2110kJ

tip You can serve the stroganoff over any favourite pasta, or with rice or mashed potatoes.

serving suggestion Serve with panzanella (page 112), or a tossed green salad and crusty bread.

chickpea corn enchiladas

We used 16cm-round corn tortillas, which are packaged in cryovac.
Unused tortillas can be frozen in freezer bags for up to three weeks.

1 tablespoon olive oil
1 small onion (80g), chopped coarsely
1 clove garlic, crushed
1 teaspoon sweet paprika
1/2 teaspoon ground chilli powder
1 teaspoon ground cumin
400g can tomato puree
300g can chickpeas, rinsed, drained
1 tablespoon coarsely chopped fresh coriander
8 corn tortillas
1 small red onion (100g), chopped coarsely
1 medium tomato (190g), chopped coarsely
1 small avocado (200g), chopped coarsely
1/2 cup (60g) coarsely grated cheddar cheese
1/2 cup loosely packed, finely shredded iceberg lettuce

1 Heat oil in medium saucepan; cook onion and garlic, stirring, until onion softens. Add spices; cook, stirring, 2 minutes. Add puree, bring to a boil; reduce heat, simmer, stirring occasionally, 5 minutes. Add chickpeas and coriander; cook, stirring, until hot.

2 Soften tortillas in microwave oven on HIGH (100%) for 30 seconds. Divide chickpea mixture and remaining ingredients among tortillas, fold enchiladas to enclose filling.

SERVES 4

per serving 21.2g fat; 1972kJ

tip You can also soften tortillas by wrapping them in foil and heating them in a moderate oven about 5 minutes or until hot.

serving suggestion Serve with dirty rice salad (page 102).

mushroom and spinach risotto

PREPARATION TIME 10 MINUTES • COOKING TIME 25 MINUTES

Arborio, a medium-grained, pearly rice variety, is ideal for this recipe because it absorbs the stock while remaining chewy in the centre of the grain.

10g butter
1 medium brown onion (150g), chopped coarsely
1 clove garlic, crushed
2 cups (400g) arborio rice
1 cup (250ml) dry white wine
2 cups (500ml) vegetable stock
1¹/₂ cups (375ml) water
150g button mushrooms, sliced thickly
1 bunch spinach (500g), trimmed, chopped coarsely
¹/₄ cup loosely packed, coarsely chopped fresh flat-leaf parsley
³/₄ cup (60g) coarsely grated parmesan cheese

1 Place butter, onion and garlic in a large microwave-safe bowl; cook on HIGH (100%) 2 minutes or until onion softens. Add rice, stir; cook, covered, on HIGH (100%) 1 minute. Add wine, stock and the water, stir; cook, covered, on HIGH (100%) 15 minutes, stirring occasionally.

2 Add mushrooms, stir; cook, covered, on HIGH (100%) 5 minutes, or until most of the liquid is absorbed.

3 Transfer risotto to a large serving bowl; stir through spinach, parsley and cheese.

SERVES 4

per serving 8.3g fat; 2193kJ

tip You can substitute medium-grain white rice for the arborio rice.

serving suggestion Serve with rocket salad with balsamic dressing and shaved parmesan.

hokkien mee noodles

Kecap manis is Indonesian thick soy sauce which has sugar and spices added.

600g hokkien noodles
2 tablespoons vegetable oil
2 cloves garlic, crushed
2 teaspoons grated fresh ginger
3 kaffir lime leaves,
    chopped finely
1 large red capsicum (350g),
    sliced thinly
1 bunch baby bok choy (500g),
    chopped coarsely
6 green onions, chopped coarsely
1 cup (80g) bean sprouts
1 teaspoon cornflour
1/3 cup (80ml) kecap manis
2 tablespoons sweet chilli sauce
1 teaspoon sesame oil
1 tablespoon water

1 Place noodles in large heatproof bowl, cover with boiling water; stand until just tender, drain.

2 Meanwhile, heat vegetable oil in wok or large frying pan; stir-fry garlic, ginger, lime leaves, capsicum and bok choy 2 minutes or until vegetables are almost tender.

3 Add onion, sprouts and noodles; stir to combine. Blend cornflour with kecap manis, sauce, sesame oil and the water, add to wok; cook, stirring, until mixture boils and thickens slightly.

SERVES 4

per serving 11.5g fat; 1355kJ

tip You could substitute chinese cabbage or any other Asian green for the baby bok choy if it's not available.

serving suggestion Serve after a starter of soft or crispy spring rolls.

megadarra

Egyptian culinary luminary Claudia Roden recalls that her aunt would serve this dish saying: "Excuse this food of the poor." On tasting it, her guests would always respond: "Keep your food of kings and give us megadarra any day."

2 cups (400g) brown lentils
1.5 litres (6 cups) boiling water
3/4 cup (150g) long-grain
    white rice
1.25 litres (5 cups) boiling
    water, extra
1 1/2 teaspoons ground allspice
1 teaspoon ground coriander
2 teaspoons salt

CARAMELISED ONION
1/4 cup (60ml) olive oil
4 large onions (800g),
    sliced thinly
2 teaspoons sugar
1/2 cup (125ml) water

1 Place lentils and the water in large microwave-safe bowl; cook, uncovered, on HIGH (100%), 15 minutes or until lentils are just tender, drain.

2 Meanwhile, combine rice, the extra water, allspice, coriander and salt in medium saucepan. Add half of the caramelised onion mixture. Bring to a boil; reduce heat, simmer, uncovered, 12 minutes. Add lentils; simmer, uncovered, 3 minutes or until rice is just tender. Spoon megadarra into serving bowl and top with remaining caramelised onion; top with whole chives, if desired.

caramelised onion Heat oil in large frying pan, add onion and sugar; cook, stirring, 5 minutes. Add half of the water; bring to a boil. Reduce heat; simmer, uncovered, 5 minutes. Add remaining water; simmer, stirring, about 5 minutes or until onion caramelises.

SERVES 4

per serving 14.9g fat; 1914kJ

tip The lentils are cooked in the microwave oven to reduce the cooking time. You can boil them in a saucepan of water or use canned lentils.

serving suggestion Serve with pitta bread or as an accompaniment to a tagine or vegetable casserole.

cauliflower, pea and fried tofu curry

PREPARATION TIME 10 MINUTES • COOKING TIME 30 MINUTES

You will need a small cauliflower weighing approximately 1kg to make this recipe.

2 tablespoons olive oil
1 medium brown onion (150g), chopped coarsely
2 cloves garlic, crushed
900g cauliflower florets
1 teaspoon ground cumin
1/2 teaspoon ground coriander
1/2 teaspoon ground turmeric
1/4 teaspoon cayenne pepper
1 teaspoon garam marsala
400g can whole peeled tomatoes
1 cup (250ml) vegetable stock
400g firm tofu
1/4 cup (60ml) vegetable oil
1 cup (125g) frozen peas, thawed

1 Heat olive oil in large saucepan, add onion and garlic; cook, stirring, until onion softens.

2 Add cauliflower and spices; cook, stirring, 2 minutes. Add undrained crushed tomatoes and stock, stir to combine; bring to a boil. Reduce heat; simmer, covered, 10 minutes or until cauliflower softens slightly.

3 Meanwhile, cut tofu into 1cm cubes. Heat vegetable oil in medium frying pan; cook tofu, in batches, until lightly coloured and crisp on all sides, drain on absorbent paper.

4 Add tofu and peas to cauliflower curry.

SERVES 4

per serving 26.5g fat; 1422kJ

tip This recipe is best made close to serving so tofu stays crisp.

serving suggestion Serve with boiled or steamed basmati rice and sweet lassi (page 99).

risotto primavera

PREPARATION 10 MINUTES • COOKING 25 MINUTES

Primavera is the Italian word for spring and the season's freshest produce is used in this risotto, which is produced by a labour-saving covered cooking method.

20g butter
2 teaspoons olive oil
1 medium leek (350g),
   sliced thinly
1 clove garlic, crushed
2 cups (400g) arborio rice
3/4 cup (180ml) dry white wine
1 1/2 cups (375ml) vegetable stock
2 1/2 cups (625ml) water
150g sugar snap peas
300g asparagus, sliced thickly
100g yellow patty-pan
   squash, quartered
2/3 cup (50g) finely grated
   parmesan cheese
1/3 cup (80ml) cream

1 Heat butter and oil in large saucepan; cook leek and garlic, stirring, until leek softens.

2 Add rice, wine, stock and the water, bring to a boil; reduce heat, simmer, covered, 15 minutes, stirring occasionally.

3 Stir in peas, asparagus and squash; cook, covered, about 5 minutes or until rice is just tender.

4 Just before serving, stir in cheese and cream.

SERVES 4

per serving 20.4g fat; 2632kJ

tip Medium-grain rice can be used instead of arborio, if preferred.

serving suggestion Serve with flaked parmesan, crusty bread and teardrop tomato salad (page 110).

brown rice slice

PREPARATION TIME 10 MINUTES • COOKING TIME 30 MINUTES

You will need 2/3 cup (130g) raw brown rice to make approximately the required amount of cooked rice.

**1¹/₂ cups (225g) cooked
   brown rice**
**2 cups (250g) coarsely grated
   cheddar cheese**
5 eggs
250g asparagus, chopped coarsely
**1 medium red capsicum (200g),
   sliced thinly**
**70g baby spinach leaves,
   chopped coarsely**
100g fetta cheese, crumbled

1 Grease deep 19cm-square cake pan; line base and two opposite sides
   with baking paper. Preheat oven to hot.

2 Combine rice, half of the cheddar and one egg in medium bowl. Press
   rice mixture firmly over base of prepared pan. Layer asparagus, capsicum
   and spinach over rice mixture.

3 Beat remaining eggs in same bowl, add remaining cheddar and fetta;
   pour egg mixture over vegetables. Bake, uncovered, in hot oven, about
   30 minutes or until slice is firm. Stand 5 minutes before serving.

SERVES 4

per serving 34.2g fat; 2174kJ

tip This slice can be served warm or cold, so it makes a good addition
to the picnic basket.

serving suggestion The warm broccoli, capsicum and tofu salad (page 103)
would make a good accompaniment.

pumpkin, spinach and fetta frittata

PREPARATION TIME 10 MINUTES • COOKING TIME 35 MINUTES

You will need to buy a piece of pumpkin weighing approximately 800g to make this recipe.

4 cups (640g) coarsely chopped pumpkin
1 large potato (300g), chopped coarsely
125g baby spinach leaves, chopped coarsely
200g fetta cheese, crumbled
3/4 cup (90g) coarsely grated cheddar cheese
8 eggs, beaten lightly
1 small red onion (100g), sliced thinly

1 Preheat oven to very hot. Grease deep 23cm-square cake pan; line base and two opposite sides with baking paper.

2 Place pumpkin in large microwave-safe bowl, cover; cook on HIGH (100%), stirring halfway through cooking time, about 5 minutes or until just tender. Place potato in small microwave-safe bowl, cover; cook on HIGH (100%) 4 minutes or until just tender.

3 Combine pumpkin and potato in large bowl; add spinach, cheeses and egg, stir to combine. Transfer egg mixture to prepared pan. Top with onion.

4 Bake in very hot oven about 25 minutes or until firm. Stand 5 minutes before serving.

SERVES 4

per serving 30.6g fat; 2032kJ

tip If you don't have a microwave oven, boil or steam pumpkin and potato, separately, until just tender; drain.

serving suggestion Serve with a rocket or spinach salad.

zucchini and lemon pasta

PREPARATION TIME 10 MINUTES • COOKING TIME 20 MINUTES

You will need four small green zucchini (360g) and four small yellow zucchini (360g) for this recipe.
Bow tie pasta is also known as farfalle or butterflies.

375g bow ties
20g butter
3/4 cup (180ml) olive oil
1 small brown onion (80g),
   sliced thinly
2 cloves garlic, crushed
2 cups (180g) coarsely grated
   green zucchini
2 cups (180g) coarsely grated
   yellow zucchini
3 teaspoons finely grated
   lemon rind
1/3 cup (80ml) lemon juice
1/3 cup loosely packed,
   coarsely chopped chives
1/2 cup (50g) walnuts, toasted,
   chopped coarsely

1 Cook pasta in large saucepan of boiling water, uncovered, until just tender; drain.

2 Heat butter and 1 tablespoon of the oil in large frying pan; cook onion and garlic until onion softens.

3 Add zucchini; cook over high heat, stirring, until zucchini is just tender, remove from heat.

4 Add pasta to zucchini mixture with remaining oil, rind, juice, chives and nuts; toss to combine.

SERVES 4

per serving 55.1g fat; 3435kJ

tip This recipe is quick to prepare and makes an ideal supper dish. It should be made just before serving.

serving suggestion Serve with a rocket and parmesan salad.

nasi goreng

PREPARATION TIME 10 MINUTES • COOKING TIME 15 MINUTES

Nasi goreng is served for breakfast, lunch and dinner in Indonesia. You will need 11/4 cups (250g) raw rice
to make approximately the required amount of cooked rice.

1 tablespoon peanut oil
1 medium brown onion (150g),
   chopped coarsely
2 cloves garlic, crushed
1 red thai chilli, sliced thinly
250g firm tofu, chopped finely
3 cups (450g) cooked white
   long-grain rice
1/3 cup (80ml) light soy sauce
2 green onions, sliced thinly
4 eggs

1 Heat oil in wok or large frying pan; stir-fry brown onion, garlic and chilli until onion softens.

2 Add tofu; stir-fry until tofu browns lightly.

3 Add rice, sauce and green onion; stir-fry until hot and well combined.

4 Meanwhile, heat oiled medium frying pan; cook eggs, in batches, on both sides, until just cooked.

5 Divide nasi goreng among serving bowls, top each with a fried egg.

SERVES 4

per serving 14.4g fat; 1457kJ

tips The egg yolks should still be runny so they drizzle over the rice. Rice can be made a day ahead. Cover, refrigerate until required.

serving suggestion Serve with gado gado (page 100).

barley and burghul fennel pilaf

PREPARATION TIME 10 MINUTES • COOKING TIME 35 MINUTES

Pearl barley is barley with the outer husk removed.
It's available from major supermarkets and health food stores.

1 tablespoon olive oil
1 medium brown onion (150g),
  sliced thinly
2 cloves garlic, crushed
2 teaspoons caraway seeds
2 teaspoons ground cumin
2 teaspoons ground coriander
1¹/₂ cups (300g) pearl barley
2 cups (500ml) vegetable stock
2¹/₂ cups (625ml) water
1 cup (160g) burghul
2 medium red capsicums (400g)
40g butter
2 baby fennel (270g), trimmed,
  sliced thinly
¹/₃ cup (95g) yogurt

1 Heat oil in large saucepan; cook onion, garlic and spices, stirring, until onion softens.

2 Add barley; cook, stirring, 1 minute. Add stock and the water, bring to a boil; reduce heat, simmer, covered, 20 minutes.

3 Stir in burghul; cook, covered, about 10 minutes or until burghul and barley are tender.

4 Meanwhile, quarter capsicums, remove and discard seeds and membranes. Roast under grill or in very hot oven, skin-side up, until skin blisters and blackens. Cover capsicum pieces with plastic or paper for 5 minutes; peel away skin, slice thinly.

5 Heat butter in medium frying pan; cook fennel, stirring, until tender.

6 Just before serving, toss capsicum and fennel into barley mixture. Top with yogurt.

SERVES 4

per serving 17.2g fat; 2264kJ
tip Regular barley can be used instead of the pearl barley.
serving suggestion Serve with a loaf of pide and a tossed green salad.

tempeh spaghetti bolognaise

Tempeh is a protein made from fermented soy beans.

300g tempeh, chopped coarsely
1 tablespoon olive oil
1 medium brown onion (150g), chopped coarsely
2 cloves garlic, crushed
600ml bottled tomato pasta sauce
1/3 cup (95g) tomato paste
1 cup (250ml) water
1/2 cup (125ml) dry white wine
1 teaspoon coarsely chopped fresh oregano
1 teaspoon coarsely chopped fresh rosemary
1/4 cup loosely packed, finely shredded fresh basil
375g wholemeal spaghetti

1 Blend or process tempeh until mixture resembles minced meat.

2 Heat oil in medium saucepan, add onion and garlic; cook, stirring, until onion softens. Add tempeh; cook, stirring, 1 minute. Add sauce, paste, the water and wine; stir to combine. Bring to a boil; reduce heat, simmer, uncovered, stirring occasionally, 5 minutes. Add herbs; simmer, uncovered, stirring occasionally, 5 minutes.

3 Meanwhile, cook pasta in large saucepan of boiling water, uncovered, until just tender; drain. Serve pasta topped with tempeh bolognaise.

SERVES 4

per serving 11.7g fat; 2392kJ

tip This sauce can be prepared a day ahead and stored, covered, in the refrigerator until just before serving time. Reheat on the stove top or in the microwave oven.

serving suggestion Serve with shaved parmesan and a green salad.

vegeroni puttanesca

PREPARATION TIME 10 MINUTES • COOKING TIME 20 MINUTES

Puttanesca comes from the Italian word puttana, meaning whore. One version of its derivation holds that the intense fragrance of the sauce was like a siren's call to men visiting brothels. Another suggests that because it's quick to prepare, it's perfect for a working girl's supper.

375g vegeroni
1/2 cup (125ml) olive oil
4 large tomatoes (1kg),
  chopped coarsely
2 cloves garlic, crushed
1/2 cup (60g) seeded green olives,
  sliced thinly
2 tablespoons drained capers
1 tablespoon coarsely chopped
  fresh basil
1/2 cup loosely packed, coarsely
  chopped fresh flat-leaf parsley
1 red thai chilli, sliced thinly

1 Cook pasta in large saucepan of boiling water, uncovered, until just tender; drain.

2 Meanwhile, heat 1 tablespoon of the oil in medium saucepan; cook tomato and garlic, stirring, until tomato just softens.

3 Stir in pasta, olives, capers, herbs, chilli and remaining oil; cook, stirring, until heated through.

SERVES 4

per serving 30.2g fat; 2676kJ

tip You can use any type of vegeroni – multi-coloured vegetable-flavoured pasta available in many shapes – or substitute your favourite pasta.

serving suggestion Serve with crusty Italian bread and shaved or grated parmesan cheese; top with green-onion curls, if desired.

soft polenta with braised vegetables

PREPARATION TIME 15 MINUTES • COOKING TIME 15 MINUTES

Polenta is a cereal made from ground corn. Like an Italian version of mashed potatoes, it's an ideal companion for saucy dishes.

2¹/₂ cups (625ml) water
1 cup (170g) polenta
¹/₂ cup (40g) finely grated
   parmesan cheese
1 tablespoon olive oil
1 medium brown onion (150g),
   sliced thinly
1 clove garlic, crushed
200g button mushrooms, halved
2 medium green zucchini (240g),
   sliced thickly
8 medium yellow patty-pan
   squash (100g), quartered
600ml bottled tomato pasta sauce
³/₄ cup (180ml) vegetable stock

1 Bring the water to a boil in medium saucepan. Sprinkle polenta gradually into water, stirring constantly. Cover, reduce heat to low; cook, stirring occasionally, about 10 minutes or until polenta thickens. Add cheese, stir until melted.

2 Meanwhile, heat oil in medium saucepan, add onion and garlic; cook, stirring, until onion softens. Add mushrooms; cook, stirring, 3 minutes. Add zucchini and squash; cook, stirring, 2 minutes. Add sauce and stock, bring to a boil; reduce heat, simmer, covered, about 8 minutes or until vegetables are just tender.

3 Serve polenta with braised vegetables.

SERVES 4

per serving 10.5g fat; 1462kJ

tip Braised vegetables can be prepared in advance. Refrigerate, covered, and reheat just before serving.

serving suggestion Serve with a tossed green salad and crusty Italian bread, such as ciabatta.

couscous cakes with mediterranean vegetables

PREPARATION TIME 15 MINUTES • COOKING TIME 20 MINUTES (plus standing time)

Couscous, a cereal made from semolina, is a North African staple.

- 1¹/₂ tablespoons olive oil
- 1 medium red onion (170g), sliced thickly
- 3 baby eggplant (180g), sliced thickly
- 2 medium green zucchini (240g), chopped coarsely
- 250g cherry tomatoes
- 250g yellow teardrop tomatoes
- ¹/₄ cup (60ml) balsamic vinegar
- 1 clove garlic, crushed
- 1¹/₂ cups (300g) couscous
- 1¹/₂ cups (375ml) boiling water
- ¹/₄ cup (20g) finely grated parmesan cheese
- 2 tablespoons coarsely chopped fresh basil
- 60g butter

1 Heat 2 teaspoons of the oil in large frying pan; cook onion, eggplant and zucchini, stirring, until vegetables soften.

2 Stir in tomatoes, vinegar, garlic and remaining oil; cook, stirring occasionally, about 10 minutes or until tomatoes are very soft.

3 Meanwhile, combine couscous with the water in large heatproof bowl; cover, stand 5 minutes or until water is absorbed, fluffing with fork occasionally. Stir in cheese and basil.

4 Heat half of the butter in large frying pan, press half of the couscous mixture into four egg rings in pan; cook until lightly browned on both sides. Carefully remove egg rings, then couscous cakes. Repeat using remaining butter and couscous mixture.

5 Serve Mediterranean vegetables with couscous cakes.

SERVES 4

per serving 21.7g fat; 2153kJ

tip Couscous can be prepared a day ahead but the cakes should be cooked just before serving.

malaysian vegetable curry

PREPARATION TIME 15 MINUTES • COOKING TIME 15 MINUTES

Malaysian cuisine springs from many cultures – it is a heady combination of Chinese, Indian and local Malay ingredients, always with an injection of chilli. You will need a piece of pumpkin weighing about 500g for this recipe.

2 red thai chillies, chopped coarsely
2 teaspoons grated fresh ginger
3 cloves garlic, quartered
1/2 cup loosely packed,
  coarsely chopped coriander root
1/2 teaspoon ground turmeric
1/2 teaspoon ground cinnamon
3 teaspoons ground cumin
1 teaspoon coriander seeds, crushed
400g can whole peeled tomatoes
400g can coconut milk
6 kaffir lime leaves, shredded finely
25g palm sugar, shaved
2 1/2 cups (400g) coarsely
  chopped pumpkin
3 medium potatoes (600g),
  chopped coarsely
200g green beans, chopped coarsely

1 Blend or process chilli, ginger, garlic, coriander root, spices and seeds until smooth. Add undrained tomatoes, process 1 minute or until tomato mixture is well combined.

2 Transfer tomato mixture to medium saucepan. Add coconut milk, leaves and sugar, bring to a boil; reduce heat, simmer tomato and coconut mixture, uncovered, 5 minutes.

3 Add pumpkin and potato; cook, covered, about 10 minutes or until just tender. Add beans; cook 3 minutes or until tender.

SERVES 4

per serving 21.6g fat; 1628kJ

tips Curry can be made in advance. Cover, refrigerate until just before serving.
If you can't buy palm sugar, you can use 1 tablespoon raw sugar.
serving suggestion Serve with warmed roti and brown rice.

satay tofu

PREPARATION TIME 10 MINUTES • COOKING TIME 20 MINUTES

Satay is one of the mainstays of Malaysian and Indonesian kitchens. Here, it's given a high protein boost by using tofu.

2 cups (400g) jasmine rice
1/3 cup (80ml) vegetable oil
900g firm tofu, chopped coarsely
1 tablespoon peanut oil
1 clove garlic, crushed
2 teaspoons grated fresh ginger
1 medium brown onion (150g),
  chopped coarsely
1/4 cup (70g) peanut butter
1/4 cup (60ml) light soy sauce
1/4 cup (60ml) sweet chilli sauce
1/2 cup (125ml) hot water
400ml can coconut cream
1 tablespoon coarsely chopped
  fresh coriander

1 Cook rice in large saucepan of boiling water, uncovered, until just tender; drain.

2 Meanwhile, heat vegetable oil in large frying pan, add tofu; cook, in batches, stirring, until browned all over. Drain on absorbent paper.

3 Heat peanut oil in large frying pan, add garlic, ginger and onion; cook, stirring, until onion softens. Add peanut butter, sauces, the water and coconut cream. Bring to a boil; reduce heat, simmer, uncovered, about 5 minutes or until sauce thickens. Add tofu and coriander; stir to heat through. Serve satay tofu with rice.

SERVES 4

per serving 68.8g fat; 4833kJ

tip Satay sauce can be prepared a day ahead. Reheat just before serving and stir through browned tofu and coriander.
serving suggestion Serve with crispy noodle cabbage salad (page 104).

grilled stuffed mushrooms

PREPARATION TIME 10 MINUTES • COOKING TIME 25 MINUTES

You could make this recipe even faster by using instant mashed potato instead of cooking raw potatoes. If you can't buy large flat mushrooms, increase the number to give a reasonable-sized serving.

4 medium potatoes (800g), chopped coarsely
1 cup (125g) frozen peas
2 tablespoons water
1 large brown onion (200g), chopped finely
2 cloves garlic, crushed
1 red thai chilli, chopped finely
4 large flat mushrooms (600g)
2 tablespoons cream
30g butter
1/2 cup (55g) coarsely grated cheddar cheese
1/4 cup loosely packed, coarsely chopped fresh flat-leaf parsley
50g butter, melted, extra

1 Boil, steam or microwave potato and peas, separately, until tender; drain.

2 Combine the water, onion, garlic and chilli in small saucepan; cook, stirring, about 5 minutes or until onion softens.

3 Meanwhile, remove stems from mushrooms.

4 Mash potatoes, peas, cream and butter in large bowl until smooth. Add onion mixture, cheese and parsley; mix well.

5 Brush mushrooms all over with extra butter. Cook mushrooms on heated oiled grill plate (or grill or barbecue) until tender. Divide potato mixture among mushrooms. Cook under hot grill about 5 minutes or until potato is lightly browned.

SERVES 4

per serving 26.3g fat; 1775kJ

tip It is quicker and easier to fill the mushrooms if you use a piping bag.

serving suggestion Serve with warm broccoli, capsicum and tofu salad (page 103) or a simple baby spinach and tomato salad.

pumpkin tagine with date couscous

PREPARATION TIME 15 MINUTES • COOKING TIME 20 MINUTES (plus standing time)

You will need to buy a piece of pumpkin weighing about 1kg to make this dish.

2 tablespoons olive oil
1 large onion (220g),
    sliced thickly
3 cloves garlic, crushed
1/2 teaspoon ground chilli
1/2 teaspoon ground turmeric
1 teaspoon ground cinnamon
1 teaspoon ground coriander
1 teaspoon ground cumin
3 cups (750ml) vegetable stock
5 cups (800g) coarsely
    chopped pumpkin
1 cup (150g) frozen broad beans,
    thawed, shelled
1 tablespoon brown sugar
3/4 cup (120g) coarsely chopped
    seeded dates
2 tablespoons coarsely chopped
    fresh coriander

COUSCOUS

50g butter, chopped coarsely
2 cups (250g) couscous
2 cups (500ml) boiling water
1/2 cup (80g) coarsely chopped
    seeded dates
1/3 cup loosely packed, coarsely
    chopped fresh coriander

1 Heat oil in medium saucepan. Add onion, garlic and spices; cook, stirring, 3 minutes or until fragrant.

2 Add stock and pumpkin, bring to a boil; reduce heat, simmer, covered, about 10 minutes or until pumpkin is almost tender.

3 Remove lid; simmer, uncovered, 5 minutes or until pumpkin mixture thickens slightly.

4 Add remaining ingredients; cook, stirring, until heated through.

5 Serve pumpkin tagine with couscous.

couscous Combine butter, couscous and the water in large heatproof bowl, cover; stand about 5 minutes or until water is absorbed, fluffing with fork occasionally. Stir in dates and coriander.

SERVES 4

per serving 21.8g fat; 2861kJ

tip Couscous can be prepared a day ahead and refrigerated until required. Reheat in the microwave oven and stir through dates and coriander just before serving.

serving suggestion Serve with harissa, a hot North African condiment.

eggs in coconut milk curry

PREPARATION TIME 10 MINUTES • COOKING TIME 15 MINUTES

Curried eggs are filling and quick to prepare, which probably explains why there's a version of them in most Asian cuisines.

2 teaspoons vegetable oil
1 large brown onion (200g),
   sliced thinly
2 teaspoons grated fresh ginger
1/4 teaspoon ground cardamom
1 teaspoon ground turmeric
1/2 cup chilli jam
25g palm sugar, shaved
400ml can coconut milk
2 tablespoons lime juice
8 hard-boiled eggs, halved
1/2 cup loosely packed, coarsely
   chopped fresh coriander

1 Heat oil in medium frying pan. Add onion, ginger and spices; cook, stirring, 3 minutes or until onion softens. Add jam, sugar and coconut milk; bring to a boil. Reduce heat; simmer, uncovered, 10 minutes.

2 Add juice, eggs and coriander to sauce; simmer, uncovered, 2 minutes or until eggs are hot.

SERVES 4

per serving 34.5g fat; 2236kJ

tips Curry sauce can be made a day ahead. Cover, refrigerate until required. Sauce should be reheated gently. Add eggs and coriander just before serving.

If you can't buy palm sugar, you can use 1 tablespoon raw sugar.

serving suggestion Serve with plain boiled or steamed rice.

tunisian spicy nut pilaf

PREPARATION TIME 10 MINUTES • COOKING TIME 20 MINUTES (plus standing time)

Pilaf is a rice- or burghul-based dish which is found, spelled in several different ways, on many Indian, North African, Middle Eastern and Mediterranean menus.

2 tablespoons (40g) ghee
1 clove garlic, crushed
2 teaspoons ground cinnamon
pinch saffron threads
1 tablespoon ground cumin
1 tablespoon ground coriander
2 cups (400g) basmati rice
2 cups (500ml) vegetable stock
2 cups (500ml) water
2 large brown onions (400g),
    sliced thinly
2 medium carrots (240g),
    sliced thickly
¼ cup (35g) shelled
    pistachios, toasted
¼ cup (40g) pine nuts, toasted

1 Melt half of the ghee in large saucepan; cook garlic and spices, stirring, until fragrant. Stir in rice; cook, stirring, 1 minute.

2 Stir in stock and the water; bring to a boil. Reduce heat; simmer, covered, 15 minutes or until rice is just tender. Remove from heat; stand, covered, 10 minutes.

3 Meanwhile, melt remaining ghee in medium frying pan; cook onion, stirring, until onion is golden brown. Remove from pan.

4 Cook carrot in same pan, stirring, until just tender.

5 Stir onion, carrot and nuts through pilaf.

SERVES 4

per serving 23.1g fat; 2643kJ

tips Any variety of long-grain rice can be used in this recipe.
Pilaf can be made a day ahead; reheat in the microwave oven.

serving suggestion Serve with pitta bread or pide and a dip, such as sesame and butter bean or watercress and yogurt (page 25).

corn and zucchini fritters with salsa

PREPARATION TIME 10 MINUTES • COOKING TIME 10 MINUTES

If you're concerned about the fat count, use a non-stick frying pan sprayed with cooking-oil spray rather than shallow-frying the fritters.

50g butter, melted
1/2 cup (125ml) milk
3/4 cup (110g) plain flour
2 eggs, beaten lightly
210g can creamed corn
2 medium zucchini (240g), grated coarsely
vegetable oil, for shallow-frying

SALSA
3 medium egg tomatoes (225g), chopped coarsely
2 medium avocados (500g), chopped coarsely
1 small red onion (100g), chopped coarsely
2 tablespoons lime juice
2 tablespoons finely chopped fresh coriander

1 Combine butter, milk, flour and egg in medium bowl; whisk until smooth. Add corn and zucchini; mix well.

2 Heat oil in medium frying pan; cook heaped tablespoons of batter, one at a time, about 2 minutes each side or until browned both sides and cooked through. Drain on absorbent paper. Serve with salsa.

salsa Combine ingredients in a small bowl.

SERVES 4

per serving 57.6g fat; 2922kJ

tip Keep cooked fritters warm in oven until serving time.

serving suggestion To continue the Mexican accent, serve chile con queso (page 24) as an appetiser before this dish.

chinese cabbage and tofu stir-fry

PREPARATION 10 MINUTES • COOKING TIME 15 MINUTES

You will need to buy a small chinese cabbage to make this recipe.

250g dried rice noodles
2 tablespoons peanut oil
300g firm tofu, chopped coarsely
1 clove garlic, crushed
1 red thai chilli, sliced thinly
200g button mushrooms, quartered
1/3 cup (80ml) black bean sauce
1/3 cup (80ml) vegetable stock
300g finely shredded chinese cabbage
1 cup (80g) bean sprouts
3 green onions, sliced thinly
2 tablespoons coarsely chopped
   fresh coriander

1 Place noodles in medium heatproof bowl, cover with boiling water, stand until tender; drain.

2 Meanwhile, heat half of the oil in wok or large frying pan; stir-fry tofu until browned all over. Drain on absorbent paper.

3 Heat remaining oil in same wok; stir-fry garlic, chilli and mushrooms until tender. Stir in sauce and stock; bring to a boil.

4 Add cabbage; stir-fry until just wilted. Remove from heat; stir in tofu, sprouts, onion and coriander.

5 Serve noodles topped with chinese cabbage and tofu stir-fry.

SERVES 4

per serving 16g fat; 1699kJ

tip Tofu can be prepared several hours ahead; it will reheat in the final stir-frying.

serving suggestion Serve Asian mushroom broth (page 22) or hot and sour soup (page 12) as a starter before this dish.

chile con frijoles

Mexican-style beans are a mildly spiced, canned combination of red kidney or pinto beans, capsicum and tomato.

1 tablespoon olive oil
1 large red onion (300g),
  chopped coarsely
1¹/₂ teaspoons ground cumin
1 red thai chilli, chopped finely
1 small red capsicum (150g),
  chopped coarsely
420g can Mexican-style beans
1¹/₄ cups (375ml) water
2 tablespoons tomato paste
310g can corn kernels
  rinsed, drained
1 medium tomato (190g),
  chopped coarsely
2 teaspoons lime juice
¹/₄ cup loosely packed, finely
  chopped fresh coriander

1 Heat oil in large saucepan. Add onion, cumin and chilli; cook, stirring, 3 minutes or until onion softens.

2 Add capsicum, undrained beans, the water and paste; bring to a boil. Reduce heat; simmer, stirring, 5 minutes or until bean mixture thickens slightly.

3 Add corn, tomato, juice and coriander; cook, stirring, until hot.

SERVES 4

per serving 6.2g fat; 1059kJ

tip This dish can be prepared ahead and refrigerated, covered, until required. Reheat gently in saucepan or microwave oven and stir in corn, tomato, juice and coriander just before serving.

serving suggestion Serve with boiled or steamed rice, sour cream and plain or flavoured corn chips.

couscous-stuffed capsicums

Filled vegetables are common in many Middle-Eastern and eastern Mediterranean cuisines. You could use tomato, eggplant or zucchini shells instead of the capsicum.

4 large red capsicums (1.4kg)
1¹/₂ cups (300g) couscous
1¹/₂ cups (375ml) boiling water
¹/₂ cup (75g) shelled pistachios
¹/₂ cup (70g) slivered almonds, toasted
¹/₂ cup (75g) dried currants
³/₄ cup (180ml) vegetable stock
1 cup (200g) rinsed, drained, canned chickpeas
2 tablespoons coarsely chopped fresh coriander
³/₄ cup (210g) yogurt
1 lebanese cucumber (130g), grated coarsely

1 Cut off and reserve capsicum tops; remove and discard seeds and membranes. Place capsicums in large microwave-safe dish; cook, covered, on HIGH (100%) for 2 minutes, cool. Preheat oven to moderately hot.

2 Combine couscous and the water in large heatproof bowl, cover; stand 5 minutes or until water is absorbed, fluffing with fork occasionally. Add nuts, currants, stock, chickpeas and coriander to couscous; mix well.

3 Divide couscous mixture among capsicums, cover each with capsicum top. Place capsicums in oiled ovenproof dish; bake, uncovered, in moderately hot oven for 20 minutes.

4 Meanwhile, combine yogurt and cucumber in small bowl. Serve stuffed capsicums with yogurt mixture.

SERVES 4

per serving 23.2g fat; 2950kJ

tip You can prepare the couscous filling a day ahead. Cover, refrigerate until required.

serving suggestion Serve capsicums with a green salad.

vegetable kebabs with balsamic dressing

You will need to soak 12 bamboo skewers in cold water for at least an hour to prevent them from splintering and scorching over heat.

250g cherry tomatoes
1 large green capsicum (350g), chopped coarsely
6 small flat mushrooms (600g), quartered
6 yellow patty-pan squash (240g), halved
3 baby eggplant (180g), sliced thickly
3 small zucchini (270g), sliced thickly
1 medium brown onion (150g), sliced thickly
500g haloumi cheese, cubed
1/3 cup (80ml) olive oil
1/4 cup (60ml) balsamic vinegar
1 teaspoon sugar
60g baby rocket leaves

1 Thread tomatoes, vegetables and cheese onto 12 skewers.

2 Cook kebabs, in batches, on heated oiled grill plate (or grill or barbecue) until browned on all sides.

3 Meanwhile, combine oil, vinegar and sugar in screw-top jar; shake dressing well.

4 Serve kebabs on rocket leaves drizzled with balsamic dressing.

SERVES 4

per serving 40.8g fat; 2402kJ

tip You can vary the vegetables according to what's in season and personal preference.

serving suggestion Serve with crusty rolls, pide or pitta bread.

vege hot-dog cassoulet

PREPARATION TIME 15 MINUTES • COOKING TIME 25 MINUTES

Cassoulet is a traditional French dish, consisting of beans and a variety of meats and sausages. We made this recipe vegetarian-friendly by using vegetarian hot dogs, which are available at major supermarkets.

1 tablespoon olive oil
1 medium brown onion (150g),
   chopped coarsely
2 cloves garlic, crushed
1 trimmed celery stick (75g),
   chopped coarsely
1 medium carrot (120g),
   chopped coarsely
1/4 cup (60ml) dry white wine
400g can whole peeled tomatoes
1/4 cup (70g) tomato paste
1/2 cup (125ml) vegetable stock
250g packet Vege-Hotdogs,
   chopped coarsely
300g can butter beans,
   rinsed, drained
1 cup (70g) stale breadcrumbs
1/4 cup loosely packed, finely
   chopped fresh flat-leaf parsley
1 tablespoon finely grated
   lemon rind

1 Preheat oven to very hot.

2 Heat oil in medium flameproof ovenproof dish; cook onion, garlic, celery and carrot, stirring, until onion softens.

3 Stir in wine, undrained crushed tomatoes, paste and stock; bring to a boil. Stir in hot dogs and beans; sprinkle with breadcrumbs.

4 Bake, uncovered, in very hot oven about 10 minutes or until breadcrumbs brown.

5 Serve cassoulet sprinkled with combined parsley and rind.

SERVES 4

per serving 12.9g fat; 1525kJ

tip Cassoulet can be prepared a day ahead up to baking stage. Sprinkle with breadcrumbs and bake just before serving.

serving suggestion Serve with crusty bread and a tossed green salad.

snow pea and asian-green stir-fry

PREPARATION TIME 10 MINUTES • COOKING TIME 10 MINUTES (plus standing time)

You can vary the Asian greens in this recipe according to what's available at the greengrocer.

375g dried rice noodles
1 tablespoon peanut oil
1 medium brown onion (150g),
   sliced thinly
1 clove garlic, crushed
2 teaspoons grated fresh ginger
4 baby bok choy (600g),
   trimmed, halved lengthways
250g choy sum, trimmed
250g chinese broccoli,
   chopped coarsely
200g snow peas, halved
2 tablespoons light soy sauce
1/4 cup (60ml) hoisin sauce
1/4 cup (60ml) plum sauce
1/4 cup (60ml) vegetable stock
2 teaspoons sesame oil
1 tablespoon white sesame
   seeds, toasted

1 Place noodles in medium heatproof bowl, cover with boiling water, stand until just tender; drain.

2 Heat peanut oil in wok or large frying pan; stir-fry onion, garlic and ginger until onion softens.

3 Add bok choy, choy sum, broccoli and snow peas with combined sauces, stock and sesame oil; stir-fry until greens are just tender.

4 Serve stir-fry on noodles; sprinkle with seeds.

SERVES 4

per serving 11.1g fat; 1995kJ

tips Add tofu to the stir-fry if you want to boost the protein content.
You can substitute your favourite noodles for the rice noodles, if preferred.
serving suggestion Serve with chopped chilli if you like your noodles spicy.

gnocchi with roasted pumpkin and burnt butter

PREPARATION TIME 5 MINUTES • COOKING TIME 15 MINUTES

From the Italian word for dumplings, gnocchi are little balls of dough – great for soaking up pasta sauces. You will need to buy a piece of pumpkin weighing about 650g to make this recipe.

500g trimmed pumpkin
1kg gnocchi
100g butter
1 tablespoon olive oil
1 clove garlic, crushed
1 tablespoon finely shredded fresh sage

1 Preheat oven to moderate.

2 Cut pumpkin into 1cm cubes. Place on oiled oven tray; roast, uncovered, in moderate oven about 15 minutes or until just tender.

3 Meanwhile, cook gnocchi in large saucepan of boiling water, uncovered, until just tender; drain. Keep warm.

4 Melt butter with oil in medium frying pan, add garlic; cook, stirring, 2 minutes. Add sage; cook, stirring, until butter foams.

5 Combine pumpkin, gnocchi and butter mixture in large bowl, stir gently.

SERVES 4

per serving 27.8g fat; 2634kJ

tip Pumpkin can be cooked in the microwave oven to reduce cooking time.

serving suggestion Serve with a rocket salad and grated or shaved parmesan cheese.

free-form spinach and ricotta pie

PREPARATION TIME 10 MINUTES • COOKING TIME 30 MINUTES

Taking the Greek pie spanakopita as our inspiration, we've simplified the recipe by replacing the traditional fillo pastry with ready-rolled puff pastry.

200g baby spinach leaves
2 tablespoons olive oil
1 medium brown onion (150g), chopped coarsely
1 clove garlic, crushed
2 teaspoons finely grated lemon rind
1/4 cup loosely packed, coarsely chopped fresh flat-leaf parsley
1/4 cup loosely packed, coarsely chopped fresh dill
2 tablespoons coarsely chopped fresh mint
1 1/2 cups (300g) ricotta cheese
2 sheets ready-rolled puff pastry

1 Preheat oven to very hot.

2 Boil, steam or microwave spinach until just wilted; drain on absorbent paper. Squeeze out excess liquid.

3 Heat oil in small frying pan, add onion and garlic; cook until onion softens.

4 Combine spinach, onion mixture, rind, herbs and cheese in large bowl; mix well.

5 Oil two oven trays and place in oven about 5 minutes to heat. Place a sheet of pastry on each tray, divide spinach mixture between sheets, leaving a 3cm border. Using a metal spatula, fold pastry roughly over edge of filling.

6 Bake pies in very hot oven about 20 minutes or until pastry browns.

SERVES 4

per serving 36.8g fat; 2184kJ

tip For best results, use a pizza tray with holes in the base – this will make it possible to cook the pastry evenly.

serving suggestion Serve with a Greek-style salad with olives and fetta.

pad thai

PREPARATION TIME 15 MINUTES • COOKING TIME 15 MINUTES

Noodles are a popular Thai snack. For this dish, Thai cooks usually use sen lek, a 5mm-wide dried rice noodle.

375g dried rice noodles
250g firm tofu
1/4 cup (60ml) peanut oil
2 cloves garlic, crushed
1 tablespoon grated fresh ginger
2 teaspoons sambal oelek
1 stalk lemon grass, sliced thinly
2 medium carrots (240g),
   sliced thinly
2 large zucchini (300g),
   sliced thinly
3 eggs, beaten lightly
1/2 cup (135g) finely
   chopped palm sugar
1/4 cup (60ml) light soy sauce
3/4 cup (180ml) mild chilli sauce
2 cups (160g) bean sprouts
2 tablespoons coarsely chopped
   fresh coriander
1/2 cup (75g) unsalted roasted
   peanuts, chopped coarsely

1 Place noodles in large heatproof bowl, cover with boiling water, stand until just tender; drain.

2 Meanwhile, cut tofu into 2cm cubes. Heat half of the oil in wok or large frying pan; cook tofu, in batches, until browned all over. Drain on absorbent paper.

3 Heat remaining oil in same wok; cook garlic, ginger, sambal oelek and lemon grass, stirring, until fragrant. Add carrot and zucchini; cook, stirring, until vegetables are tender.

4 Add egg to wok; cook, stirring, until egg sets.

5 Stir in combined sugar and sauces; bring to a boil.

6 Add tofu, sprouts, coriander, peanuts and noodles; stir-fry until hot.

SERVES 4

per serving 33.3g fat; 3552kJ

tip If you are unable to buy palm sugar, use 1/2 cup raw sugar.

serving suggestion Serve with snow pea and Asian-green stir-fry (page 90).

mushrooms with buckwheat kernels

PREPARATION TIME 10 MINUTES • COOKING TIME 30 MINUTES

This recipe is inspired by the Russian passion for kasha, dishes made from cooked grains such as buckwheat, millet or oats. Buckwheat kernels are available from health food stores.

60g butter
1 large onion (200g),
   chopped finely
11/2 cups (260g) buckwheat kernels
21/2 cups (625ml) vegetable stock
2 tablespoons olive oil
250g button mushrooms,
   sliced thinly
250g flat mushrooms,
   sliced thinly
150g oyster mushrooms,
   sliced thinly
2 cloves garlic, crushed
1/3 cup loosely packed, coarsely
   chopped fresh chives

1 Heat half of the butter in small saucepan, add onion; cook, stirring, 2 minutes or until onion softens. Add buckwheat and stock; bring to a boil. Reduce heat; simmer, covered, 10 minutes. Remove lid; simmer, uncovered, 5 minutes or until liquid is absorbed and grains are tender.

2 Meanwhile, heat remaining butter and oil in large frying pan. Add mushrooms and garlic; cook, stirring, 10 minutes or until mushrooms are tender and juices evaporate. Combine buckwheat with mushroom mixture. Stir in chives just before serving.

SERVES 4

per serving 24.4g fat; 2092kJ

tip Substitute any mushroom variety for the ones specified.

serving suggestion Serve with potato and beetroot salad (page 107).

drinks

For a refreshing breakfast in a glass, a nutritious serving of extra fruit and vegies, or merely a thirst quencher, these quick-mix drinks are just the thing.

pawpaw, orange, lime and pineapple juice

PREPARATION TIME 10 MINUTES

You will need about half a medium pawpaw and a third of a small pineapple to make this recipe. Use the leftovers as the basis of a fruit salad.

400g trimmed pawpaw
3 medium oranges (720g)
1 medium lime (80g)
130g trimmed pineapple

1 Chop peeled fruit coarsely.

2 Blend or process fruit until smooth.

SERVES 4 (MAKES 1 LITRE)

per 250ml serving
0.3g fat; 391kJ

tip Add some fresh mint for extra flavour.

serving suggestion Serve with toasted fruit bread spread with ricotta and honey.

beetroot, apple and ginger juice

PREPARATION TIME 10 MINUTES

This colourful drink makes a great pick-me-up at any time of day.

11 large green apples (2.2kg), cored, chopped coarsely
1 large beetroot (200g), peeled, chopped coarsely
5cm piece fresh ginger, chopped coarsely

1 Push ingredients through juice extractor; stir to combine.

SERVES 4 (MAKES 1 LITRE)

per 250ml serving
0.5g fat; 878kJ

tip If you don't own a juice extractor, blend or process ingredients until smooth, then push the mixture through a fine sieve into a jug.

serving suggestion Serve as a breakfast drink or as a zingy accompaniment to salad sandwiches or wraps.

mixed melon and strawberry juice

PREPARATION TIME 10 MINUTES

You will need half a medium honeydew melon and a quarter of a round watermelon to make this recipe.

525g trimmed honeydew melon
650g trimmed watermelon
250g strawberries

1 Chop melons coarsely.

2 Push ingredients through juice extractor; stir to combine.

SERVES 4 (MAKES 1 LITRE)

per 250ml serving
0.8g fat; 378kJ

tips If you don't own a juice extractor, blend or process ingredients until smooth, then push the mixture through a fine sieve into a jug.

Rockmelon can be substituted for honeydew, if preferred.

serving suggestion Serve over crushed ice.

beetroot, apple and ginger juice

almond milk

PREPARATION TIME 10 MINUTES

Almond milk has been around since medieval times, when it was developed as a nutritious and soothing substitute for fresh animal milk – which is hard to keep without refrigeration.

2¹/₂ cups (400g) blanched almonds, toasted
1.25 litres (5 cups) iced water
3 teaspoons vanilla essence

1 Blend or process ingredients until smooth.

2 Strain mixture through a piece of fine muslin cloth; squeeze out excess liquid into large jug. Discard almond pulp.

SERVES 4 (MAKES 1 LITRE)

per 250ml serving
55g fat; 2488kJ

tip Almond pulp can be used in breakfast cereal or, if you prefer, as a great facial scrub.

serving suggestion This is a good accompaniment to serve with vegan dishes.

carob soy shake

PREPARATION TIME 5 MINUTES

Carob is a natural chocolate substitute available from health food stores in light and dark powder as well as in block form.

1 litre (4 cups) soy milk
2 tablespoons carob powder
2 teaspoons cinnamon
2 teaspoons caster sugar

1 Blend or process ingredients until smooth.

SERVES 4 (MAKES 1 LITRE)

per 250ml serving
7.1g fat; 646kJ

tip Drinking chocolate can be substituted for carob powder, if preferred.

serving suggestion Serve with blueberry bagels spread with cream cheese and topped with berries.

sweet lassi

PREPARATION TIME 5 MINUTES

In Indian kitchens lassi is made with buttermilk as well as yogurt, and both sweet and salty versions are served with savoury dishes.

1 small mango (300g), chopped coarsely
2 cups (500g) yogurt
1¹/₂ cups (375ml) iced water
2 tablespoons caster sugar

1 Blend or process ingredients until smooth.

SERVES 4 (MAKES 1 LITRE)

per 250ml serving
4.4g fat; 640kJ

tip Vary the fruit according to the season.

serving suggestion Sweet lassi makes great breakfast fare.

salads

gado gado

Gado gado is Indonesian in origin. You can vary the salad ingredients to include cauliflower, cucumber or fresh pineapple pieces.

5 cups (400g) finely shredded white cabbage
200g green beans
375g firm tofu
vegetable oil, for deep-frying
2 large tomatoes (500g)
1 cup (80g) bean sprouts
4 hard-boiled eggs, quartered

PEANUT SAUCE
¾ cup (210g) crunchy peanut butter
¼ cup (60ml) water
2 tablespoons light soy sauce
2 tablespoons sweet chilli sauce
½ cup (125ml) coconut milk

1 Boil, steam or microwave cabbage and beans, separately, until just tender; drain. Rinse under cold water; drain.

2 Cut tofu into 2cm pieces. Heat oil in wok or large frying pan; deep-fry tofu until browned lightly. Drain on absorbent paper.

3 Cut each tomato into eight wedges. Arrange cabbage, beans, tofu, tomato, bean sprouts and egg on large platter; serve with peanut sauce.

peanut sauce Combine ingredients in medium saucepan; cook, stirring, over medium heat until sauce is smooth.

SERVES 4

per serving 53.7g fat; 2909kJ

tip Peanut sauce can be made a day ahead and refrigerated, covered; reheat just before serving.

serving suggestion Serve with boiled or steamed rice or nasi goreng (page 64).

dirty rice salad

PREPARATION TIME 15 MINUTES • COOKING TIME 10 MINUTES

The combination of rice and red beans, straight out of America's Deep South, is given a new twist in this salad.

2 cups (400g) medium-grain white rice

1 small red onion (100g), chopped coarsely

2 trimmed sticks celery (150g), sliced thinly

1 small red capsicum (150g), chopped coarsely

400g canned borlotti beans, rinsed, drained

1/3 cup (50g) pine nuts, toasted

1 teaspoon ground cumin

1/2 teaspoon cayenne pepper

1/4 cup (60ml) lemon juice

1 tablespoon balsamic vinegar

1 Cook rice in large saucepan boiling water, uncovered, until just tender; drain. Rinse rice under cold water; drain.

2 Combine rice and remaining ingredients in large bowl; mix well.

SERVES 4

per serving 10g fat; 2325kJ

tip You can cook the rice a day ahead and refrigerate, covered, until ready to assemble the salad.

serving suggestion Serve with corn bread or muffins.

warm broccoli, capsicum and tofu salad

PREPARATION TIME 20 MINUTES • COOKING TIME 10 MINUTES

The tofu in this salad makes it substantial enough to serve as a main course.

600g broccoli florets
2 large red capsicums (700g)
180g firm tofu
1/3 cup (80ml) olive oil
1 teaspoon sesame oil
2 tablespoons balsamic vinegar
1 clove garlic, crushed
**2 teaspoons sesame
  seeds, toasted**

1 Boil, steam or microwave broccoli until just tender; drain. Rinse under cold water; drain.

2 Quarter capsicums; remove and discard seeds and membranes. Roast under grill or in very hot oven, skin-side up, until skin blisters and blackens. Cover capsicum pieces with plastic or paper for 5 minutes. Peel away skin; chop capsicum coarsely. Cut tofu into 1cm cubes.

3 Combine remaining ingredients in screw-top jar; shake well.

4 Combine vegetables, tofu and dressing in large bowl; toss gently.

SERVES 4

per serving 23.9g fat; 1279kJ

tip Salad can be prepared several hours in advance and refrigerated, covered, until just before serving.

serving suggestion Serve with pide or other flat bread.

crispy noodle cabbage salad

PREPARATION TIME 15 MINUTES

*Crunchy or fried noodles are available round or flat
– either can be used in this salad.*

3 cups (240g) finely shredded cabbage
3 cups (240g) finely shredded red cabbage
300g packet crunchy noodles
8 green onions, chopped finely
**1/2 cup loosely packed, finely chopped
    fresh flat-leaf parsley**
2 tablespoons sesame seeds, toasted

DRESSING
1 tablespoon sesame oil
1 tablespoon peanut oil
2 tablespoons white vinegar
2 tablespoons light soy sauce
1/2 cup (125ml) sweet chilli sauce

1 Place cabbages, noodles, onion, parsley and seeds in large bowl.

2 Pour over dressing; toss to combine.

dressing Combine ingredients in screw-top jar; shake well.

SERVES 4

per serving 22.8g fat; 1464kJ

tips Make this salad just before serving or the noodles will lose
their crispness.

The dressing can be made ahead of time and refrigerated.

serving suggestion Serve with grilled or barbecued tofu.

bean thread vermicelli salad

PREPARATION TIME 15 MINUTES • COOKING TIME 5 MINUTES

Bean thread noodles (also known as mung bean or green bean noodles or vermicelli), cloud ear mushrooms and tamari are all available at Asian grocery stores. If not available, normal rice vermicelli can be substituted, dried shiitake mushrooms or fresh mushrooms may be used and light soy sauce can take the place of the tamari.

100g bean thread noodles
120g snake beans,
   chopped coarsely
3 dried cloud ear mushrooms
1 medium tomato (190g),
   halved, sliced thinly
1 small red onion (100g),
   sliced thinly
1 clove garlic, crushed
1 small red thai chilli,
   chopped finely
2 tablespoons lime juice
2 tablespoons tamari
1 tablespoon coarsely chopped
   fresh coriander

1 Place noodles in medium heatproof bowl, cover with boiling water; stand until just tender, drain. Boil, steam or microwave beans until just tender; rinse under cold water, drain.

2 Place mushrooms in small heatproof bowl, cover with boiling water; stand 5 minutes, drain. Slice mushrooms thinly.

3 Combine noodles, beans, mushrooms, tomato and onion in medium bowl; toss gently with combined remaining ingredients.

SERVES 4

per serving 0.5g fat; 430kJ

tip Noodles and mushrooms can be soaked several hours ahead; drain. Refrigerate, covered, until ready to assemble salad.

serving suggestion Accompany with a Thai-style green papaya salad to make a good, low-fat, low-joule summer meal.

potato and beetroot salad

PREPARATION TIME 10 MINUTES • COOKING TIME 15 MINUTES

This update on a Russian classic makes a colourful addition to the salad buffet.

3 large potatoes (750g)
1 small fresh beetroot (90g)
1/3 cup (40g) frozen peas
3 hard-boiled eggs, quartered
3/4 cup (210g) yogurt
1 tablespoon coarsely chopped
fresh dill
1 tablespoon coarsely chopped
fresh flat-leaf parsley
2 large dill pickles,
chopped coarsely
1 small red onion (100g),
chopped finely

1 Boil, steam or microwave potatoes until just tender; drain. Cool; cut into 2cm cubes.

2 Boil, steam or microwave beetroot and peas, separately, until just tender; drain. Cool; chop beetroot coarsely.

3 Combine potato, beetroot, peas and remaining ingredients in medium bowl; toss salad gently.

SERVES 4

per serving 6.2g fat; 1017kJ

tips Canned whole baby beets can be substituted for fresh beetroot, if preferred.

Potatoes, beetroot and peas can be cooked in advance and refrigerated, covered. Combine salad just before serving or beetroot will "bleed" into egg and potato.

serving suggestion Serve as an accompaniment to grilled or barbecued vegetables, such as eggplant, kumara and zucchini.

tabbouleh with chickpeas

PREPARATION TIME 15 MINUTES (plus standing time)

Made with fresh parsley, mint and burghul (crushed processed wheat kernels), tabbouleh is a cornerstone of Middle-Eastern cuisine. You will need about three bunches of flat-leaf parsley for this recipe.

1/2 cup (80g) burghul
3 cups loosely packed, coarsely
   chopped fresh flat-leaf parsley
3 medium tomatoes (570g),
   chopped finely
1 small red onion (100g),
   chopped finely
1 cup loosely packed, coarsely
   chopped fresh mint
300g canned chickpeas,
   rinsed, drained
1/2 cup (125ml) lemon juice
1/4 cup (60ml) olive oil

1 Cover burghul with water in small bowl; stand about 10 minutes or until burghul softens. Drain in fine strainer; squeeze out excess liquid.

2 Meanwhile, combine parsley, tomato, onion, mint and chickpeas in large bowl; add burghul.

3 Toss salad gently with combined juice and oil.

SERVES 4

per serving 15.5g fat; 1149kJ

tip Parsley can be chopped using scissors.

serving suggestion Serve with pitta bread and hummus or tahini.

rice salad

PREPARATION TIME 10 MINUTES • COOKING TIME 12 MINUTES

Any type of rice can be used for this salad; you could even try a blend of wild and basmati rices.

2 cups (400g) white
   long-grain rice
2 lebanese cucumbers (260g),
   seeded, sliced thinly
1 large carrot (180g),
   grated coarsely
2 large oranges (600g),
   peeled, sliced thinly
100g snow pea tendrils
1 cup (100g) toasted pecans,
   sliced lengthways
1/4 cup loosely packed,
   finely shredded fresh mint

DRESSING
2 tablespoons red wine vinegar
1/4 cup (60ml) olive oil
2 teaspoons sugar

1 Cook rice in large saucepan of boiling water, uncovered, until just tender; drain. Rinse rice under cold water; drain.

2 Combine rice with remaining ingredients in large bowl.

3 Pour over dressing; toss to combine.

dressing Combine ingredients in screw-top jar; shake well.

SERVES 4

per serving 37.1g fat; 3300kJ

tip Rocket can be substituted for snow pea tendrils, if preferred.

serving suggestion Serve salad in lettuce or witlof leaves.

teardrop tomato salad

Any type of pesto can be used in the dressing.

500g asparagus, trimmed, halved
250g cherry tomatoes, halved
500g yellow teardrop tomatoes, halved
100g rocket leaves
2 small avocados (400g), sliced thickly
1/3 cup loosely packed, finely shredded fresh basil

DRESSING
1/3 cup (80ml) olive oil
1 tablespoon white vinegar
1 tablespoon basil pesto
1 clove garlic, crushed

1 Boil, steam or microwave asparagus until just tender; drain. Rinse under cold water; drain.

2 Combine asparagus, tomatoes, rocket, avocado and basil in large bowl.

3 Pour dressing over tomato salad; toss gently.

dressing Combine ingredients in screw-top jar; shake well.

SERVES 4

per serving 36.5g fat; 1562kJ

tip Asparagus can be prepared in advance and refrigerated, covered, until just before assembling salad.

serving suggestion Serve with crusty Italian bread.

panzanella

PREPARATION TIME 15 MINUTES • COOKING TIME 10 MINUTES

Panzanella is a traditional Italian bread salad that probably came about as a way of using up yesterday's bread. For this recipe, we used ciabatta, a wood-fired white loaf readily available from most supermarkets, but any Italian crusty bread may be used in its place.

1/2 long loaf ciabatta
4 medium tomatoes (760g),
  chopped coarsely
2 lebanese cucumbers (260g),
  chopped coarsely
1 medium red onion (170g),
  chopped coarsely
1 cup (120g) seeded black olives
1 tablespoon drained capers
1 clove garlic, crushed
1/4 cup (60ml) tomato juice
2 tablespoons red wine vinegar
2 tablespoons olive oil
2 tablespoons coarsely chopped
  fresh flat-leaf parsley
2 tablespoons coarsely chopped
  fresh basil

1 Preheat oven to moderately hot.

2 Cut bread into 2cm cubes. Place bread on oven tray; bake, uncovered, in moderately hot oven about 10 minutes or until crisp.

3 Combine bread with tomato, cucumber, onion, olives, capers and garlic in large bowl.

4 Just before serving, toss panzanella mixture with combined remaining ingredients.

SERVES 4

per serving 11.5g fat; 1366kJ

tip Bread can be prepared a day ahead and stored in an airtight container.

serving suggestion Serve as a substantial starter or an accompaniment to a pasta main course.

spiced lentil salad

PREPARATION TIME 15 MINUTES • COOKING TIME 15 MINUTES

1 cup (200g) brown lentils
1 cup (200g) red lentils
150g sugar snap peas
250g fresh asparagus,
  sliced thickly
2 trimmed sticks celery (150g),
  sliced thinly
4 green onions, chopped finely
1/2 small red onion (50g),
  sliced thinly
2 teaspoons olive oil
1 tablespoon ground cumin
1 tablespoon ground coriander
2 teaspoons sweet paprika
1/2 cup (140g) yogurt
2 teaspoons finely grated
  lemon rind
1/4 cup (60ml) lemon juice

1 Cover brown lentils with water in medium saucepan; bring to a boil. Reduce heat; simmer, covered, about 15 minutes or until lentils are tender, drain. Rinse under cold water; drain.

2 Meanwhile, cover red lentils with water in medium saucepan; bring to a boil. Reduce heat; simmer, covered, about 5 minutes or until lentils are just tender, drain. Rinse under cold water; drain.

3 Boil, steam or microwave peas and asparagus, separately, until just tender; rinse under cold water, drain.

4 Combine lentils, peas, asparagus, celery and onions in large bowl. Heat oil in small saucepan; cook spices, stirring, until fragrant. Stir spice mixture, yogurt, rind and juice into lentil mixture; toss together.

SERVES 4

per serving 6.3g fat; 1518kJ

tips Undressed lentil salad can be made a day ahead. Cover, refrigerate until just before serving.

Canned brown lentils can be substituted for the dried lentils, if preferred.

serving suggestion Serve salad in pitta pockets or warmed roti or chapati (Indian bread).

tempeh larb

PREPARATION TIME 20 MINUTES

Larb is a tangy Thai salad usually served as part of a banquet, though it could be served as a stand-alone dish.

600g tempeh, chopped finely
1 tablespoon finely grated
**   lime rind**
1/3 cup (80ml) lime juice
1 red thai chilli, sliced thinly
2 shallots, sliced thinly
4 green onions, sliced thinly
1/3 cup loosely packed, coarsely
**   chopped fresh mint**
1 tablespoon finely chopped
**   lemon grass**
4 small iceberg lettuce leaves

1 Combine tempeh, rind, juice, chilli, shallot, onion, mint and lemon grass
   in large bowl; mix well.

2 Divide larb mixture among lettuce leaves.

SERVES 4

per serving 7.6g fat; 925kJ

tip Larb can be made a day ahead and refrigerated, covered.

serving suggestion Serve with wedges of cucumber and tomato,
and top with green-onion curls.

glossary

allspice also known as pimento or Jamaican pepper; available whole or ground.

almonds, blanched almonds with brown skins removed.

beans

BORLOTTI also known as roman beans; eaten fresh or dried, and available in cans. Pale-pink or beige beans with darker red spots; a good substitute for pinto beans.

BUTTER cans labelled butter beans are, in fact, cannellini beans. Butter beans is also another name for lima beans.

BROAD also known as fava beans, these are available fresh, canned and frozen. Fresh, these are best peeled twice (discarding both the outer long green pod and the sandy-green inner shell).

CANNELLINI small white beans; sold in cans as butter beans.

MEXICAN-STYLE commercially canned product of either pinto or red kidney beans with capsicum and spices.

REFRIED pinto beans (similar to borlotti), cooked twice: soaked and boiled then mashed and fried, traditionally in lard. A Mexican staple, "frijoles refritos" (refried beans) are available canned.

beetroot also known as red beets or beets; firm, round root vegetable.

bran, unprocessed made from the outer layer of a cereal, most often the husks of wheat, rice or oats.

breadcrumbs, stale one- or two-day-old bread made into crumbs by grating, blending or processing.

buckwheat seeds are roasted and used whole or made into flour; substitute cracked wheat.

butter use salted or unsalted ("sweet") butter; 125g is equal to one stick of butter.

burghul also known as bulghur wheat; hulled steamed wheat kernels that are dried and crushed into grains.

carob powder cocoa substitute.

capsicum also known as bell pepper or, simply, pepper.

cheese

CHEDDAR the most common cow milk "tasty" cheese; should be aged, hard and have a strong flavour.

FETTA Greek in origin; a crumbly textured goat- or sheep-milk cheese with a sharp, salty taste.

FONTINA Italian in origin; semi-hard cheese with brown or red rind and nutty flavour.

HALOUMI firm cream-coloured sheep-milk cheese; tastes like a minty fetta. Haloumi can be grilled or fried briefly.

PARMESAN a dry hard cheese made from skim or part-skim milk; the best, from Italy – grana padano or reggiano – are aged at least three years.

PIZZA CHEESE a commercial blend of grated mozzarella, cheddar and parmesan.

RICOTTA a sweet, fairly moist, fresh curd cheese with a low fat content.

chickpeas also called garbanzos, hummus or channa; an irregularly round, sandy-coloured legume.

chilli

JALAPENO sold chopped or whole in vinegar, as well as fresh; we used the medium-hot, sweetish chopped, bottled version.

THAI small, hot chilli; dark-green to bright-red in colour.

chinese green vegetables the following vegetables go by more than one name; we have listed the alternatives.

BOK CHOY (bak choy, pak choi, chinese white cabbage, chinese chard) fresh, mild mustard taste; use stems and leaves. Baby bok choy is a smaller, more-tender variety.

CHINESE BROCCOLI also known as gai larn or Chinese kale.

CHOY SUM also known as flowering bok choy or flowering white cabbage.

coriander also known as cilantro or Chinese parsley; bright-green leafy herb.

corn thins packaged popped corn crispbread, available from supermarkets.

couscous North African in origin; fine, grain-like cereal product made from semolina.

dashi fish and seaweed stock used in Japanese cooking; made from dried bonito flakes and kelp (konbu). Instant dashi powder, also known as dashi-no-moto, is a concentrated powder sold in Asian food stores.

eggplant also known as aubergine.

eggs some recipes in this book call for raw or barely cooked eggs; exercise caution if there is a salmonella problem in your area.

galangal also known as laos; a root with a piquant peppery flavour that is a member of the ginger family; used fresh or dried and ground.

garam masala ground-spice blend; includes cardamom, cinnamon, clove, coriander, fennel and cumin.

ghee clarified butter; with the milk solids removed, this fat can be heated to a high temperature without burning.

ginger, pickled thin, light-pink shavings of ginger pickled in vinegar; Japanese in origin. Available, bottled, from Asian grocery stores.

japanese pepper also known as sansho; a hot Japanese seasoning ground from the pod of the prickly ash tree.

kaffir lime leaves aromatic leaves of a small citrus tree bearing a wrinkle-skinned yellow-green fruit.

kecap manis also spelled ketjap manis; Indonesian thick soy sauce which has sugar and spices added.

kumara Polynesian name of orange-fleshed sweet potato often confused with yam.

lemon grass tall, clumping, lemon-smelling and -tasting, sharp-edged grass; use white lower part of the stem.

lentils (red, brown, yellow) dried pulses often identified by and named after their colour; also known as dhal.

melons

ROCKMELON round melon with orange flesh; also known as a cantaloupe.

HONEYDEW round melon with delicate taste and pale-green flesh.

milk we used full-cream homogenised milk unless otherwise specified.

BUTTERMILK (1.8g fat per 100ml) sold alongside fresh milk products in supermarkets; low in fat. Originally the liquid left after butter was churned, today, it is made similarly to yogurt.

SKIM MILK POWDER we used dried milk powder with 1% fat content when dry and 0.1% when reconstituted.

SOY non-dairy product made from pressed soy beans. It is higher in protein than cow milk and is cholesterol-free, low in calcium, fat and sodium.

broad beans

baby bok choy

bok choy

brown miso

white miso

hokkien noodles

miso made in Japan, miso is a paste made from cooked, mashed, salted, fermented soy beans; available in red and white, although "red" is dark brown and "white" is the colour of weak tea.

muesli also known as granola, a combination of grains, nuts and dried fruits.

mushrooms

BUTTON small, cultivated white mushrooms with a delicate, subtle flavour.

ENOKI clumps of long, spaghetti-like stems with tiny, snowy-white caps.

OYSTER also known as abalone mushrooms; has fan-shaped fluted cap and ranges in colour from pearly white to cream, peach and grey.

SHIITAKE also known as donko or chinese mushroom; often sold dried – soak to rehydrate before use.

STRAW cultivated Chinese mushroom; usually sold canned in brine.

SWISS BROWN also known as roman or cremini; light- to dark-brown mushroom with full-bodied flavour.

noodles

BEAN THREAD also known as bean thread vermicelli, or cellophane or glass noodles; soak in boiling water to soften.

FLAT RICE fresh soft white noodles made from rice flour.

FRIED crispy egg noodles packaged (commonly a 100g packet) already deep-fried and sometimes labelled crunchy noodles.

HOKKIEN also known as stir-fry noodles; fresh wheat flour noodles resembling thick, yellow-brown spaghetti. Must be rinsed under hot water to remove starch and excess oil.

DRIED RICE dried noodles made from rice flour; available flat and wide or thin (vermicelli). Should be soaked in boiling water to soften. Also known as rice stick noodles.

WHEAT a dried wheat-flour noodle; available flat or very thin, and fresh or dried.

onion

GREEN also known as scallion or (incorrectly) shallot; an immature onion with a long, bright-green edible stalk.

RED also known as spanish, red spanish or bermuda onion; a sweet-flavoured, large, purple-red onion.

SHALLOT formed more like garlic covered with a thin papery skin. The skin colour ranges from pale brown to dark rose.

SPRING have crisp, narrow green-leafed tops and a smallish round white bulb.

pearl barley barley which has had its outer husk (bran) removed, and been steamed and polished.

pepitas dried pumpkin seeds.

pide also known as turkish bread; comes in long, flat loaves and individual rounds. Made from wheat flour.

pitta often referred to as lebanese bread; sold in large flat pieces that separate into two thin rounds.

polenta a flour-like cereal made of ground corn (maize); coarse-textured cornmeal. Also the name of the dish made from it.

preserved lemon quartered lemons preserved in lemon juice and salt. To use, remove and discard pulp, squeeze juice from rind, rinse rind well then slice thinly. Sold singly or in jars at delicatessens; once open, store in refrigerator.

saffron stigma of a member of crocus family; available in strands or ground form. Store in the freezer.

sambal oelek (also ulek or olek) Indonesian in origin; a salty paste made from ground chillies and vinegar.

sugar we used coarse granulated table sugar, also known as crystal sugar, unless otherwise specified.

PALM very fine sugar from the coconut palm. It is sold in cakes, also known as gula jawa, gula melaka and jaggery. Substitute with raw, brown or black sugar.

tahini a rich, buttery paste made from crushed sesame seeds; used in making hummus and other Middle-Eastern sauces.

tamari a thick, dark soy sauce made mainly from soy beans, without the wheat used in standard soy sauce.

tempeh produced by a natural culture of soy beans; has a chunky, chewy texture.

tiny taters canned tiny new potatoes.

tofu also known as bean curd; an off-white, custard-like product made from the "milk" of crushed soy beans. Comes fresh as soft or firm, and processed as fried or pressed dried sheets.

tortilla thin, round unleavened bread which originated in Mexico; can be made at home or purchased frozen, fresh or vacuum-packaged. Two kinds are available, one made from wheat flour and the other from corn (maizemeal).

vege hot dogs packaged, precooked vegetable protein hot dogs. Made from a mixture of wheat gluten, soy proteins, potato starch and rice flour. Available in supermarkets.

vegeroni vegetable-flavoured, multi-coloured pasta in various shapes.

wakame a deep-green edible seaweed. It is available in fresh or dried forms from Asian supermarkets.

wheat germ flakes milled from the embryo of wheat.

zucchini also known as courgette.

dried rice noodles

tempeh

index

make your own stock

This recipe can be made up to 4 days ahead and stored, covered, in the refrigerator. If the stock is to be kept longer, it is best to freeze it in smaller quantities. *This recipe makes about 2.5 litres (10 cups).*

Stock is also available in cans or tetra packs. Stock cubes or powder can be used. As a guide, 1 teaspoon of stock powder or 1 small crumbled stock cube mixed with 1 cup (250ml) water will give a fairly strong stock. Be aware of the salt and fat content of stock cubes and powders and prepared stocks.

VEGETABLE STOCK

2 large carrots (360g), chopped
2 large parsnips (360g), chopped
4 medium onions (600g), chopped
12 sticks celery, chopped
4 bay leaves
2 teaspoons black peppercorns
6 litres (24 cups) water

Combine ingredients in large saucepan; simmer, uncovered, 1 1/2 hours, strain.

facts and figures

Wherever you live, you'll be able to use our recipes with the help of these easy-to-follow conversions. While these conversions are approximate only, the difference between an exact and the approximate conversion of various liquid and dry measures is minimal and will not affect your cooking results.

liquid measures

metric	imperial
30ml	1 fluid oz
60ml	2 fluid oz
100ml	3 fluid oz
125ml	4 fluid oz
150ml	5 fluid oz (¼ pint/1 gill)
190ml	6 fluid oz
250ml	8 fluid oz
300ml	10 fluid oz (½ pint)
500ml	16 fluid oz
600ml	20 fluid oz (1 pint)
1000ml (1 litre)	1¾ pints

dry measures

metric	imperial
15g	½oz
30g	1oz
60g	2oz
90g	3oz
125g	4oz (¼lb)
155g	5oz
185g	6oz
220g	7oz
250g	8oz (½lb)
280g	9oz
315g	10oz
345g	11oz
375g	12oz (¾lb)
410g	13oz
440g	14oz
470g	15oz
500g	16oz (1lb)
750g	24oz (1½lb)
1kg	32oz (2lb)

helpful measures

metric	imperial
3mm	⅛in
6mm	¼in
1cm	½in
2cm	¾in
2.5cm	1in
5cm	2in
6cm	2½in
8cm	3in
10cm	4in
13cm	5in
15cm	6in
18cm	7in
20cm	8in
23cm	9in
25cm	10in
28cm	11in
30cm	12in (1ft)

measuring equipment

The difference between one country's measuring cups and another's is, at most, within a 2 or 3 teaspoon variance. (For the record, one Australian metric measuring cup holds approximately 250ml.) The most accurate way of measuring dry ingredients is to weigh them. When measuring liquids, use a clear glass or plastic jug with the metric markings. (One Australian metric tablespoon holds 20ml; one Australian metric teaspoon holds 5ml.)

how to measure

When using graduated metric measuring cups, shake dry ingredients loosely into the appropriate cup. Do not tap the cup on a bench or tightly pack the ingredients unless directed to do so. Level top of measuring cups and measuring spoons with a knife. When measuring liquids, place a clear glass or plastic jug with metric markings on a flat surface to check accuracy at eye level.

Note: North America, NZ and the UK use 15ml tablespoons. All cup and spoon measurements are level.

We use large eggs having an average weight of 60g.

oven temperatures

These oven temperatures are only a guide. Always check the manufacturer's manual.

	°C (Celsius)	°F (Fahrenheit)	Gas mark
Very slow	120	250	½
Slow	140-150	275-300	1-2
Moderately slow	170	325	3
Moderate	180-190	350-375	4-5
Moderately hot	200	400	6
Hot	220-230	425-450	7-8
Very hot	240	475	9

nutritional guide

The nutritional counts listed in this table apply to a single main course serving.

	LOW	MEDIUM	HIGH
Fat (g)	0-15	15-30	30+
Cal	0-300	300-600	600+
kJ	0-1254	1254-2508	2508+
Carb (g)	0-30	30-60	60+
Protein (g)	0-20	20-40	40+
Fibre (g)	0-10	10-20	20+

Looking after **your interest...**

Keep your ACP cookbooks clean, tidy and within easy reach with slipcovers designed to hold up to 12 books. *Plus* you can follow our recipes perfectly with a set of accurate measuring cups and spoons, as used by *The Australian Women's Weekly* Test Kitchen.

To order

Mail or fax Photocopy and complete the coupon below and post to ACP Books Reader Offer, ACP Publishing, GPO Box 4967, Sydney NSW 2001, or fax to (02) 9267 4967.

Phone Have your credit card details ready, then phone 136 116 (Mon-Fri, 8.00am-6.00pm; Sat, 8.00am-6.00pm).

Price

Book Holder
Australia: $13.10 (incl. GST).
Elsewhere: $A21.95.

Metric Measuring Set
Australia: $6.50 (incl. GST).
New Zealand: $A8.00.
Elsewhere: $A9.95.
Prices include postage and handling.
This offer is available in all countries.

Payment

Australian residents We accept the credit cards listed on the coupon, money orders and cheques.

Overseas residents We accept the credit cards listed on the coupon, drafts in $A drawn on an Australian bank, and also British, New Zealand and U.S. cheques in the currency of the country of issue. Credit card charges are at the exchange rate current at the time of payment.

Test Kitchen
Food director *Pamela Clark*
Food editor *Karen Hammial*
Assistant food editor *Amira Ibram*
Test Kitchen manager *Cathie Lonnie*
Home economists *Sammie Coryton, Nancy Duran, Benjamin Haslam, Elizabeth Macri, Christina Martignago, Sharon Reeve, Susie Riggall, Jessica Sly, Kirrily Smith, Kate Tait*
Editorial coordinator *Rebecca Steyns*
Nutritional information *Laila Ibram*

ACP Books
Editorial director *Susan Tomnay*
Creative director *Hieu Chi Nguyen*
Senior editor *Julie Collard*
Designer *Michele Withers*
Studio manager *Caryl Wiggins*
Sales director *Brian Cearnes*
Publishing manager (rights & new project *Jane Hazell*
Marketing director *Nicole Pizanis*
Sales and marketing coordinator *Caroline*
Pre-press *Harry Palmer*
Production manager *Carol Currie*
Business manager *Seymour Cohen*
Business analyst *Martin Howes*
Chief executive officer *John Alexander*
Group publisher *Pat Ingram*
Publisher *Sue Wannan*
Editor-in-chief *Deborah Thomas*

Produced by ACP Books, Sydney.
Printed by Dai Nippon Printing in Korea.
Published by ACP Publishing Pty Limited 54 Park St, Sydney; GPO Box 4088, Sydney, NSW 2001.
Ph: (02) 9282 8618 Fax: (02) 9267 9438
acpbooks@acp.com.au
www.acpbooks.com.au
To order books, phone 136 116.
Send recipe enquiries to:
recipeenquiries@acp.com.au
AUSTRALIA: Distributed by Network Se GPO Box 4088, Sydney, NSW 2001.
Ph: (02) 9282 8777 Fax: (02) 9264 327
UNITED KINGDOM: Distributed by Aust Consolidated Press (UK), Moulton Park Business Centre, Red House Rd, Moulton Park, Northampton, NN3 6AQ.
Ph: (01604) 497 531 Fax: (01604) 497 5
acpukltd@aol.com
CANADA: Distributed by Whitecap Book 351 Lynn Ave, North Vancouver, BC, V7J
Ph: (604) 980 9852 Fax: (604) 980 819
customerservice@whitecap.ca
www.whitecap.ca
NEW ZEALAND: Distributed by Netlink Distribution Company, ACP Media Centr Cnr Fanshawe and Beaumont Streets, Westhaven, Auckland.
PO Box 47906, Ponsonby, Auckland, NZ
Ph: (09) 366 9966 ask@ndcnz.co.nz
SOUTH AFRICA: Distributed by PSD Promotions (Pty) Ltd, PO Box 1175, Isand 1600, Gauteng, Johannesburg, SA.
Ph: (011) 392 6065 Fax (011) 392 6079
orders@psdprom.co.za

Vegetarian meals in minutes
Includes index.
ISBN 1 86396 238 7

1. Vegetarian cookery. 2. Quick and easy cooking. I. Australian Women's We (Series: Australian Women's Weekly Home Library).
641.5636
© ACP Publishing Pty Limited 2001
ABN 18 053 273 546
This publication is copyright. No part of may be reproduced or transmitted in an form without the written permission of th publishers.
First published 2001. Reprinted 2004 (tv

Photocopy and complete coupon below

☐ **Book Holder**

☐ **Metric Measuring Set**
Please indicate number(s) required.

Mr/Mrs/Ms _____

Address _____

_____

Postcode _____ Country _____

Ph: Business hours ( ) _____

I enclose my cheque/money order for $ _____
payable to ACP Publishing.

OR: please charge my

☐ Bankcard ☐ Visa ☐ Mastercard

☐ Diners Club ☐ American Express

Card number

Expiry date ____ /____

Cardholder's signature _____

Please allow up to 30 days delivery within Australia.
Allow up to 6 weeks for overseas deliveries.
Both offers expire 31/12/05. HLVEG05